# BUSINESS BUILDER'S BLUEPRINT

## THE PROVEN FORMULA FOR GREATER COMPANY SUCCESS

WALL STREET JOURNAL BESTSELLING AUTHOR

## ALLEN E. FISHMAN

# TABLE OF CONTENTS

# DEDICATION

*To Jonathan, for his courage,*
*which is such an inspiration to those who know him.*

# PREFACE

Earlier in my career I was trained to use traditional strategic planning. When I say traditional, I mean the type of strategic planning that is very effective for very large companies. These companies have the deep infrastructure needed to devote the large amount of time that is required to make traditional planning effective. I worked for a multi-billion dollar company that had top-level executives who had the time needed to focus on such strategic planning. But, as I started working with small and midsized businesses, it quickly became apparent that traditional strategic planning does not work for them. That's why I developed a strategic planning process that had amazingly positive results with small and midsized businesses. The results of the process were:

- Greater profits

- All employees from management on down working in alignment to achieve the business owner's vision

- Less stress for the business leaders

In 1987, I decided to "bottle" my strategic planning process so that other small and midsized businesses could benefit from it. During the next three years, I documented my process, which I referred to as Business Builder's Blueprint (Blueprint) to make it easy for small and midsized businesses to be run strategically. I refer to this process as the Blueprint throughout this book.

This resulted in an easy-to-use methodology for strategic planning which, with the assistance of someone trained in the process, helps business owners achieve their personal and company visions. Blueprint includes a very specific implementation program that involves not just the business owner, but also those in the company who report directly to the business owner. Blueprint focuses on everything needed to succeed - from the clear identification of the company vision through driving the various strategic plans down to the lowest level of the organization.

In 1990, I created The Alternative Board (TAB), which has grown into the world's largest franchise system providing peer advisory board and coaching services for business owners, as well as alignment training for those who report to them. One of the fundamental benefits TAB provides to small and midsized businesses is helping them do their strategic planning using the Business Builder's Blueprint process.

My goal for Business Builder's Blueprint is to help you to identify your personal and company long-term visions of success and to help make these dreams of yours come true.

*Allen Fishman*

# ACKNOWLEDGEMENTS

I'd like to thank those in the worldwide TAB Community who helped to create the Business Builder's Blueprint. Even though it is true that business owners from different countries, and even different parts of the same country, are different from each other with different cultures and political ideologies; it is also true that the great majority of the challenges and opportunities they face are the same. It's very gratifying that the methods and tools shared in this book have proven to be universally valuable to business owners, and their companies, across the globe.

TAB is the world's largest franchise system providing peer advisory and coaching services to business owners. TAB Boards, as of 2018, are operating in nearly 20 countries around the world.

I would particularly like to thank Michele Fishman and Dana Besbris for their contributions to making this book happen. I am grateful to them, as well as Dave Scarola and Joe Schumacher for embracing my original ideas and taking them so much farther.

I developed the Blueprint process and the original toolset based on my own experience helping business owners run their small and medium-sized businesses more strategically.

TAB is a global village in the truest sense and our Facilitator/Coaches have contributed immensely to using and enhancing the Blueprint process and toolset, challenging me and contributing their very best thinking to pushing the boundaries of what's possible.

As I've traveled and met TAB Members from around the world, it has been heartwarming to hear so many members open their hearts in sharing with me how using Business Builder's Blueprint has benefited not only their companies, but also them personally in making their visions come true. I am truly touched that TAB membership and Blueprint have become such an important part of their businesses and their lives.

# ELEMENT 1: PERSONAL AND COMPANY VISION STATEMENTS
# INTRODUCTION

Business Builder's Blueprint (BBB) is a dynamic process that will help you to strategically lead your business to the next level and beyond. There are four distinct process elements, each of which will certainly be beneficial if used individually, but when used together, will have an amazing synergistic impact on your life and your ability to lead your business to reach your vision of success. The elements consist of the following:

- **Personal and Company Vision Statements**

- **The Look in the Company Mirror**

- **Company Plans**

- **Making it Happen**

This section, Element 1, focuses on the first element of Blueprint, which is identifying the destination that you, the business owner, want for your future. As a business owner, your desired vision for the future must be aligned with the reality of your business, as well as its future. Creating a clear picture of your dreams before the plans are made will make it more likely that your plans will succeed. Only when this alignment exists will your best chance of reaching your unique long-term vision of success be achieved.

Blueprint will help you to develop a clear picture of that future, which I refer to as your Personal Vision, and your long-term dreams of success for your company, which I refer to as your Company Vision. Only after you have identified your Personal Vision and Company Vision will you be able to create the most effective path to achieve your long-term visions.

Knowing and using these two aligned visions will create less stress and more happiness, and an overall harmonious fusion of your business and personal life.

As important as it is to identify your Personal and Company Visions, it is equally important to articulate those visions into clearly defined statements. Blueprint accomplishes this with the written 100-Word Statements, designed to easily translate your Personal and Company Visions into words.

## WRITTEN 100 WORD STATEMENTS

A central component used in Blueprint is the creation of 100-word written statements, to assist with the key areas that need to be very clearly and succinctly identified. The written Personal and Company Vision Statements do not need to be works of literary greatness. On the contrary, all that is needed is a series of clear and articulate bullet points in order to manifest each of the Vision Statements.

Before your 100-word written Personal and Company Vision

Statements are finalized, we advise that you tap the advice of external advisors with whom you are open to sharing your dreams. They may challenge your statements by adding another perspective. For those who are TAB Board members, the TAB Board and TAB-Certified Facilitator Coach will be additional resources for challenging and advising you on your formal written Vision Statements, as well as your other written company statements that are not part of Element 1.

## NO EXCUSES

We know from experience that many new TAB business owner members see the benefits of Blueprint's strategic planning, but still manage to come up with excuses for not embracing it as a central part of their personal and company culture. Let's look at some of the most common excuses that business owners use when they want to put off creating a blueprint for their business. I hope that you will see that none of the excuses should keep you from making strategic planning an integral part of your culture.

## EXCUSE ONE: I NEED TO FOCUS ON A MAJOR COMPANY CHALLENGE RIGHT NOW

Business owners find it easy to put off creating their blueprint because they manage their businesses by perpetually staying in the putting-out-the-daily-company-"fires" mode. I have heard countless new business owner members tell me, "I can't start my Blueprint right now; my business is facing challenges and I need to focus on them." This is actually a reason to begin using Business Builder's Blueprint! The great thing about Blueprint is that by identifying your most critical short-term company challenges (and with the help of the Blueprint system), you can start immediately using Blueprint to develop a plan to solve those problems now.

By identifying and addressing an immediate crisis, you'll find that you don't have to stay in the rut of running your business from a day-to-day perspective. Blueprint can help you easily break out of this daily crisis management mode and jump-start your use of Blueprint by seeing very quick results from the effort.

## EXCUSE TWO: I AM MORE "HANDS-ON" THAN STRATEGIC BY NATURE

CEOs of large publicly owned businesses are almost totally involved in the larger, strategic level of the businesses they own and work for; conversely, owners of small businesses are frequently more hands-on. The smaller the business, the more likely the owner is consumed with the detailed, day-to-day tactical aspects of running the company.

The Blueprint process reflects an understanding that you, the business owner, are the driving force of your business, and as such, will likely have a deep hands-on involvement. Regardless, in order to maximize the short-term survival and long-term success of your company, it is essential that you move the majority of your focus away from the day-to-day aspects of operating your company. Blueprint provides simple-to-use methods and tools to shift your focus to strategically leading your business, while still being able to attend to your tactical involvement. Regardless of the size of your business, using the Blueprint process will help you move away from constantly "putting out fires" to creating room for you to be more strategically proactive and less reactive in leading.

## EXCUSE THREE: I DON'T WANT TO BE ACCOUNTABLE TO ANYONE ELSE

Blueprint requires and creates accountability to projected results that have been agreed upon. Some business owners find this challenging because one of the reasons they go into business in the first place is so that they will not have to be accountable to anyone else. Business owners don't have accountability to anyone in their businesses and rarely have any accountability to a board of directors in the way that a CEO of a publically owned company must.

On the downside, without accountability to projected results, your company is less likely to attain your vision of success. Blueprint encourages and supports you to put yourself on the line for all to see that you believe that certain results will happen, as well as giving yourself the extra incentive to make sure the results happen.

## EXCUSE FOUR: MY COMPANY DOESN'T HAVE THE RESOURCES TO ALLOCATE THE TIME

Blueprint will create – rather than absorb – employee time. It reduces wasted or misdirected time and helps eliminate your employees' ineffective use of time. Instead, you will maximize return on your human resource investments. Implementing Blueprint enables your management and non-management employees to focus on what is best for your company. This results in less fragmentation of employee time and efforts into areas that are not critical to the success of your business.

You are not expected, when using Blueprint, to divert your employees' "bandwidth" from working on their day-to-day responsibilities in order to focus on strategic planning. Blueprint can be adapted to the human resource infrastructure of any company, regardless of its size. The type of reviews done weekly in large companies, for example, may be adapted to a monthly basis if your business is a smaller company.

## EXCUSE FIVE: I'VE TRIED STRATEGIC PLANNING AND IT DIDN'T WORK

Many TAB members have tried traditional, strategic planning before joining TAB, and it didn't work for them. The reason traditional strategic planning has a history of failure when applied to privately owned businesses is because "traditional" strategic planning was developed to work well for large, publicly owned companies with decentralized divisions and functions. Sheer size dictated a need to structure the planning process. In contrast, Blueprint was developed very intentionally to work just for privately owned businesses, which as we all know, are operated as a different kind of business animal.

Even though our TAB members are unique and come from diverse backgrounds with different experiences and planning skills, applying Blueprint to businesses has been easy for them because the principles of Blueprint work effectively for all types and sizes of private businesses.

## EXCUSE SIX: MY COMPANY IS VERY SUCCESSFUL

Blueprint is right for your company regardless of the current level of success or lack thereof. If your company is already successful, Blueprint will help your company achieve its full potential. The Blueprint process will give you new insights into how to lead your company to achieve its full potential.

One of the biggest reasons for early failure is that many companies encounter major problems due to rapid growth without proper controls. These problems can be avoided if Blueprint is used to manage the growth. Companies experiencing very rapid growth who utilize Blueprint experience an increase in employee efficiency because of the protocols and controls that come with the use of Blueprint. These same companies eliminate wasted employee time doing activities not aligned with the goals of the company.

## EXCUSE SEVEN: MY COMPANY IS FACING TOUGH ECONOMIC TIMES

If your company is facing tough economic times or is in sheer survival mode, this is not the time to delay using Blueprint "until things get better." Businesses that are struggling economically often need a course change to get through their economic struggles. The Blueprint process is the perfect vehicle to develop these course changes. It will give you the strategic tools to make sure your company identifies the essential changes needed, and the tools to carry out those changes most effectively during economic and business fluctuations. Blueprint will provide your company with the tools needed to be efficient in using your available resources to successfully fight through tough economic times and move past survival mode to your desired level of success.

CASE STUDIES

# MAKING IT HAPPEN FOR DIFFERENT SIZE COMPANIES

Business Builder's Blueprint must be used differently to work best for different size companies. I will show you how to customize the Making It Happen process to the size of your company. To help you understand how to strategically lead your particular size business, three case studies are showcased, each of which involves different size companies that track how they applied Blueprint to their businesses. These three different size case study companies are referred to throughout the book and are generically described in the following ways:

- Small-size companies refer to companies with less (even significantly less) than $1 million in annual revenue.

- Mid-size companies refer to companies with more than $1 million in sales and less than $10 million in annual revenue.

- Large-size companies refer to companies with more than $10 million in annual revenue.

The three case studies, based upon company annual revenue size, involve composites of different business owners and their businesses to illustrate points. Because of confidentiality, which is so integral to the entire TAB peer Board/Coaching dynamics, the names of the individuals, their companies, and even their industries have been changed for the purpose of the case studies.

The Blueprint process easily adapts to any size company to help bring about your greater success. Throughout this book I will show how the Blueprint process adapts to each of three different size companies. These case studies will help you understand how each of the business owners used this process to make their companies reach the dreams they had for their companies. The following is a brief overview of each of these three different size case study companies.

**SMALL-SIZE COMPANY:**

Arden Construction, a small contract construction company, was founded and is owned by Andrew Arden. The company grossed approximately $750,000 in annual revenue for 2007, but its revenue fell to approximately $500,000 during the two years following the great recession that same year. Arden Construction has six employees including a job supervisor and an office manager; the company makes heavy use of subcontractors.

The company's founder and owner, Andrew Arden, is a member of TAB, with similar size small businesses members referred to as Entrepreneur Boards. Members running small businesses are typically very active in the day-to-day aspects of their business. There is great limitation on management infrastructure in these small-size companies, if there are any management employees at all. Blueprint, used at its most basic level for small businesses, can still bring about the fullest benefits.

Andrew Arden is married and has one teenage boy. He has the desire to build his company to a level where he can personally take out a minimum income of at least $100,000 a year. He enjoys the hands-on aspects of knowing what is happening at every level of his business, such as supply purchases, timely deliveries and benchmarks on project completions that are being done to his specifications. He has no desire to manage a large number of employees, nor does he care to grow the company to a size that will require him to manage a large organization.

Andrew was presented with the opportunity to obtain a government construction contract that would have doubled Arden Construction's profits, but would have also resulted in needing to add a large number of employees to fulfill the contract. Given his expressed goals, he passed on the opportunity. Despite the attraction and prestige associated with the contract, he didn't want his company to infringe too much on his personal time and his desire for a flexible schedule.

Andrew views his construction company as more than just a source of income for him and his family. He truly cares about providing on-time, high-quality construction services and wants his company to reflect his personal integrity. Andrew enjoys working with like-minded employees who are passionate about the benefits of his company's services. He has even stitched onto his employee uniforms the words that most represent his business philosophy: Affordable, On-time, High Quality Construction, and the words are also affixed on his company vehicle.

Andrew believes very strongly in the importance of referral business coming from satisfied clients. To help bring this about, he pays for training for his employees to teach them how to provide a high level of customer service, a training that is unusual for small-size construction companies.

Arden Construction's greatest strength is Andrew's knowledge of quality construction. But, like many small business owners, he has a problem with taking on too many tasks and not being able to get them all done and it has had an impact on his health and relationships. He tries to focus 75 percent of his work time on activities that make the most of his strengths, and all his other work-related activities to 25 percent or less. His company's greatest weakness is its dependence on Andrew for new business. Most new business comes from referrals of previous satisfied clients or people Andrew has met or by networking with large general contractors in the area.

Despite being a young man, Andrew Arden suffered two heart attacks within a few months of one another. As a result, he is trying to lose weight and get in better shape. He recently started a routine of working out and walking for an hour during lunchtime. He hopes these changes to his lifestyle will help him lose 40 pounds and, as a result, avoid future heart problems.

The threat of future heart problems has also led Andrew to make the decision to train his supervisor to take over some of Andrew's responsibilities, appointing the supervisor to be his successor if Andrew were to become incapacitated or die. This also had the effect of helping counter Andrew's problem of taking on too many tasks and not being able to get them all done. The transfer of responsibility has also helped to relieve some of the extreme stress that was partially responsible for his health concerns. Through this process he was able to then reduce his time at work to a four-and-a-half-day workweek.

## MID-SIZE COMPANY:

The Baker Fabrication Company, a metal fabrication manufacturer, grosses $2.5 million in annual revenue and has a team of experienced management and manufacturing personnel. The company has 20 employees, including two executives, two mid-level managers, as well as a sales manager and a controller who reports to Bridget Baker, the owner. The company has a well-documented manufacturing system and owns patents on certain products and parts. Bridget personally owns the company headquarters and fabrication building, which has the capacity to be expanded for a great amount of growth.

Bridget is a member of a TAB Board that includes mid-size members in a board referred to as a Presidents Board. Members running mid-size companies are not able to commit the same time and resources on the number of Company Plans that large-size companies can commit to; they do incorporate the same Blueprint strategic planning principles while focusing on only one or two Company Plans.

Sean Baker, Bridget's father, founded Baker Fabrication. Several years before his death, Sean had delegated most of his CEO-type work responsibilities to Bridget. Sean Baker was in his mid-80s and was still working part-time in the Baker Fabrication business when he died. Shortly before he died, Sean had withdrawn from most day-to-day business activities, but still spent 20-30 hours a week on the specific business projects that he enjoyed.

Bridget enjoys using her outstanding selling ability and allocates much of her time on business development with large account prospects.

Bridget has a husband, two daughters and two young grandsons from one of her daughters. Neither of her daughters is interested in joining the business.

Bridget's family life is very important to her and she wants to maximize her time with her family, so she plans her workday so she can be home at dinner with her husband every evening. Bridget's mother is still alive and independent, but at 90 years old, Bridget anticipates a future time when she will need to devote more time to care for her.

Bridget enjoys going to her grandchildren's sporting competitions and taking family vacations. Some days, Bridget leaves early from work, in order to be at her grandkids' games. She also spends time with them during their school breaks and enjoys taking them skiing; she doesn't want to lose the ability to take several weeks a year off to do these things with her family.

Bridget has decided against a strategy that would involve expanding into an out-of-town regional sales office because she doesn't want to increase her own traveling. She also doesn't want to take on the financial risk of an additional office without direct "hands-on" involvement in its success.

Bridget has a dream of retiring within ten years with enough money to live comfortably. To fund her retirement, Bridget has a long-term plan of selling Baker Fabrication and upon retirement, she plans to pursue her love of painting, traveling the world, and spending more time with her grandkids. She does not share her dream to sell the business with her managers, out of concern they would quit if they knew her long-term intentions for the business.

## LARGE-SIZE COMPANY:

Conroy Technology, an IT consulting company, grosses $20 million in annual revenue. The company has fifty employees including two brothers, Doug and Mark Conroy who own it, five executives and eight non-executive level managers. The company uses Blueprint to its fullest extent with a management infrastructure committed to strategic planning and to the full implementation of the planning process. The two brothers use the Blueprint leadership methods to lead their company towards making their Company Vision a reality.

The father of the brothers, Sam, was the founder of Conroy Technologies. Conroy Technologies has two divisions, a software division and a hardware division. Several years ago, at the time of Sam's death, Doug managed the software division and Mark managed the hardware division. The two synergistic divisions share general overhead such as the accounting and marketing departments.

Before their father's death, Doug and Mark Conroy had worked for several years as Conroy Technologies' top two executives and reported directly to their father. Sam also had a third son who did not have any interest in the family business. Sam wanted Doug and Mark to work in the business and had for years, told them that they would eventually own the business equally, when Sam died, the two brothers did received equal ownership of the business.

Mark Conroy is a member of a TAB Board, which is called a Strategic Board because it includes large businesses like Conroy Technologies that have the infrastructure to allow their owners to focus a substantial amount of their time on strategic matters. After becoming co-owner of Conroy Technologies, Mark identifies to his TAB Board that he wants to spend more time developing Conroy Technologies' strategic direction, negotiating deals and building relationships with clients that are central to the revenue of Conroy Technologies. Serving as the company's COO, Mark expresses a desire to turn over those responsibilities to one of the Hardware Division company managers and take over the CEO role of Conroy Technologies. His personal long-term vision includes a more minor involvement in day-to-day business activities, particularly things such as personnel issues. During his free time, Mark likes to spend time sailing.

Doug Conroy is very active with his local Rotary Club and he often travels out of town in order to fulfill his Rotary responsibilities, which negatively impacts his work commitment to the family business. Doug wants to retire within the next five to ten years.

At times it has been very challenging for the brothers to be in alignment on key factors concerning the future of the company, their respective responsibilities, and how the company should be operating.

# PERSONAL VISION STATEMENT

The unique vision an individual business owner has may not include maximizing profits or potential selling price. These desires may involve such things as family benefits, image in the community, flexibility of time away from office, and so many other items that are not profit-oriented. Blueprint connects what the owner wants the business to bring to his/her personal life and helps make these things happen, even if company success for the business owner means something other than maximizing profits.

Like most business owners, your business is much more to you than just your "job." For many, including me, our self image is tied to being "the owner of the business." I am often reminded of this when I think of comments made by Sam Conroy, founder of Conroy Technologies, our large company example, when he leaned forward on the board room table during a TAB Board meeting, splayed his hands out as if grabbing the table and said, "Well, I just received an amazing offer – an unsolicited one – to buy out my company." He then mentioned the price, which involved millions of dollars.

Many of the TAB members eyes widened, thinking, how wonderful this was for Sam. "But," Sam said, leaning back, "I'm not going to take it." One of his fellow TAB members asked him why. Sam Conroy answered, "I know it's an extremely generous offer." He hesitated, and then said, "But, my business is me and I am my business; there is no separating us." Many of his fellow TAB members nodded their heads in mutual understanding. For most business owners, their company is one of the most important aspects of their lives, and its purpose and emotional value to the business owner is very important. Money matters, but it isn't everything.

Before you can start to strategically lead your business, you have to know where you want to go, in order to get it to where you want your business to be. Unless you know this destination, your business leadership style will waste your and others' time and work efforts because of a lack of direction. Everything within your business should be leading toward attaining your Personal Vision, which is your dream for your long-term future.

Personal Visions are long-term and usually constant. However, life happens and Personal Visions change. Events such as the birth of a child, a divorce, the death of a loved one and health challenges sometimes cause modifications to Personal Vision Statements, and are covered later in the section entitled "Turning the Blueprint Wheels." The first Blueprint process step for you as a business owner, however, should be creating your written Personal Vision Statement. I said "should be" because, as I will discuss later in this book, many have started the Blueprint process by first addressing other matters critical to their companies.

If there are multiple owners of your business, the Personal Vision Statements of each of the owners need to be written, and the business-related factors need to be shared with each other. The owners must try hard to find alignment on key areas that can lead to satisfying the most important emotional needs of each of the owners. Without alignment, the results can be damaging to the relationship and the business will underachieve. In extreme cases, these unresolved conflicts may cause the disintegration of the business. If your company has multiple owners, pay very close attention to Chapter 6, which shows how Business Builder's Blueprint applies to companies with multiple owners.

Identify in your Personal Vision Statement your "wants" versus your "needs." If your want is great, and you don't get it, you can still find the happiness and success you desire. You may want a company jet, but know your company will never be able to support the cost, so you will still be able to live a happy life if you don't get one. However, if your need is great, and you don't satisfy it, chances are you won't find the happiness you seek.

Your written Personal Vision Statement should include the key factors in your long-term dreams for your desired future. To develop your Personal Vision Statement, you will need to identify what constitutes long-term success and a satisfying life for you. What type of life, five to ten years from now, would make you smile and say, "I am living my dreams"?

Later in this book you will see how the factors expressed in your Personal Vision Statement impact your Company Vision Statement, which in turn impacts on all major company decisions.

## KEY NON-EXIT STRATEGY FACTORS TO CONSIDER WHEN CRAFTING YOUR PERSONAL VISION STATEMENT:

To clarify your dreams for the future of your business, I've identified critical factors to consider the priorities of non-exit strategy factors. These include the following, and we'll discuss each:

- Material lifestyle

- Willingness to put personal assets at risk

- Personal passion for what you do

- Time away from work

- Where your business is located

- Out of town work travel

- Family members employed in the business

### MATERIAL LIFESTYLE

For most business owners, desired material lifestyle is one of the first factors mentioned. This involves receiving material rewards from their business, including compensation, benefits and perks. This factor typically impacts significantly on the destination business owners want for their business and the role the business needs to play in their lives. What are your material lifestyle dreams? Is this material lifestyle realistically attainable in the future through the financial results of your business?

Your business attaining the maximum possible profits may not be the most important destination to you. Andrew Arden, our small business owner, for example, has a long-term dream that includes taking out a specific minimum six-figure income from his contracting company. He doesn't care about growing the company to create income growth opportunities beyond this amount.

When I created TAB in 1990, my desires for what I hoped to receive from TAB included, and still include, things that go far beyond the organization being a vehicle for making money. For example, my Personal Vision Statement stated a desire for TAB to become a major agent for positive change among business owners. Knowing that TAB makes a difference to thousands of TAB business owner members provides me with a great emotional reward.

## WILLINGNESS TO PUT PERSONAL ASSETS AT RISK

Business owners are often required to personally guarantee loans or leases for their company. Many business owners have the desire to eliminate these personal guarantees. If this is an important thing for you, you should express this in your Personal Vision Statement.

## PERSONAL PASSION FOR WHAT YOU DO

As Thomas Carlyle wisely warned, "A man without a purpose is like a ship without a rudder." The level of passion business owners have for their businesses is typically great if what they are primarily doing, is work they enjoy doing. This passion keeps them powering their companies' vision to the finish line, even when things are tough. The reality is that business owners have a high level of passion for driving their company to their definition of great success.

Passion for what you do is the key factor in keeping you enthused to drive your company to reach your dreams. Therefore, it should not be surprising that under the Blueprint process, your personal passions are the first factors to consider in creating your Personal Vision Statement.

What would you ideally like to be doing at your business? Many business owners, at times, dread going to work because their work requires them to be involved in many things they don't enjoy. But the good news is that you have "pull" with the boss of your company, since you are the boss. You can make changes so you are doing the activities you enjoy and have the aptitude for as your primary function in the day-to-day business.

Andrew Arden enjoyed very hands-on type work involvement with his small contractor company, Arden Construction. He didn't want to manage many employees beyond his current six employees. He wanted to continue using subcontractors because he did not have to engage them for the next project if he was unhappy with them on a current project.

In contrast, Mark Conroy, COO of Conroy Technologies, identified his desire for the following work responsibilities in his Personal Vision Statement:

- **Spend more time developing Conroy Technologies' strategic direction, negotiating deals and building relationships with large companies that can provide a major impact.**

- **Get out of COO type work for the division I currently run, to a pure CEO role, with only minor involvement in day-to-day business and personnel activities.**

Mark's Personal Vision Statement resulted in a Company Plan for Conroy Technologies that resulted in his transition from his then current CEO/COO role, to more of a pure CEO role for the division of the company that he ran. This process took over three years to accomplish and included such things as developing his Director of Operations to take over as COO, so that Mark could stop being involved with projects that didn't directly match his passion.

## TIME AWAY FROM WORK

The time spent away from the business doing non-work related activities must be accounted for in your Personal Vision Statement. Being able to make the decision about how much time to spend annually away on vacation or to work a flexible work schedule is one of the great things about being a business owner and shouldn't be ignored. Nor should it become a source of self-provoked guilt. Personal values and interests should shape your dream of how you want to spread your time between work time and non-work time.

Many business owners have a tendency to get so obsessed with their business that they live too much of their lives in their "business owner role" and don't plan for enough time away from work to balance their lives. Make sure your dreams for the future of your company and your time commitment to your company are a realistic match. What you decide will greatly influence such things as the growth plans you develop for your business.

Andrew Arden is a scratch two golfer. His long-term dream included coming in late a few days a week during golf season to practice. He not only loves to improve his game, but the sport keeps him fit and happy. Every business owner needs to make sure to plan your time away from work for physical activity, which will help with your stress level, an important factor for personal health as well as helping to manage your business more effectively. Andrew Arden articulated in his Personal Vision Statement that in addition to golf, he wanted to have a routine of working out during long lunch hours, in order to lose 40 pounds and to avoid further heart problems and to stave off his family's medical history of diabetes. These factors resulted in a Company Plan to provide coverage for him during the time he would not be available for work.

Doug Conroy, the other co-owner of Conroy Technologies, became very active with his local Rotary Club and traveled to fulfill these Rotary responsibilities. He identified this involvement with Rotary as a spiritual commitment when writing his Personal Vision Statement. His responsibilities to Conroy Technologies was greatly impacted by the amount of time committed to his spiritual life; Mark, like Doug, reflected in his Personal Vision Statement his long-term desire to spend time away from work to sail, which was also important to his overall well-being. Their business will need to accommodate both partners' personal visions, and the Blueprint process will allow this happen.

The midsize business owner, Bridget Baker, created a Personal Vision Statement that included spending family time going to her grandkids' school and sports competitions, including their practices. Her Personal Vision identified being home at dinner with her husband every evening as a top priority. She now leaves work early some days, or takes school breaks off in order to spend important time with her grandchildren and extended family. She also defined that in the future she would need to create the necessary time and space to care for her elderly mother.

## WHERE YOUR BUSINESS IS LOCATED

There is no right or wrong answer for where you want to live and work; there's only what is right for you. Where you want your business to be located should be part of your Personal Vision Statement. You might want to move your business to an area you love because of a particular climate or terrain or because it would be closer to where you live. For example, years ago, I identified that it was important to me that the TAB offices be moved closer to the Foothills in Boulder County, which are many miles outside Denver, because I live in the Foothills on a part-time basis. A plan was developed for finding an office building much closer to my home. In 2007, a 28,000 square foot office building was purchased to be TAB's headquarters.

## OUT-OF-TOWN WORK TRAVEL

The amount of out-of-town business travel you want to be doing should be part of your Personal Vision Statement. Out-of-town business travel affects life quality and requires plans for having your absence at work covered by others. Bridgette Baker's Personal Vision Statement expressed her desire to maximize time spent with her family. She decided against any additional out-of-town regional sales office expansion because she wanted to decrease the amount of travel required for business purposes.

## FAMILY MEMBERS EMPLOYED IN BUSINESS

A desire to employ family members in the business is an important factor for many business owners and should be included your Personal Visions Statement. If your Personal Vision Statement includes employing a family member who is not currently employed in the business, consider whether that desire is something you will share with your employees, or whether it is a Pocket Factor that you will not share with your employees. A Pocket Factor is a part of your Personal Vision that you may not want to show or share with others – think of your Pocket Factor as keeping something in your pocket rather than having it out to show.

Be aware that family business relationships present special challenges. If your business employs family members, or if you are considering employing family members, I recommend that you read my book, "9 Elements of Family Business Success," published by McGraw Hill.

# PERSONAL VISION STATEMENT:
# EXIT STRATEGY FACTORS

Bridget Baker had a dream of retiring within ten years with enough money to live comfortably financially. Her vision involved using the money for her retirement which would remain from the after-tax proceeds of the sale of her business. Upon retirement, she planned to pursue her love of painting, travel the world, and spend more time with her grandkids. Bridget initially identified her exit strategy in her Personal Vision Statement, but chose to not share the strategy with her executives because she didn't want them to worry about their own job security, which might lead them to start looking for positions with other companies.

At some point, your Personal Vision Statement will most likely express your desire to either cut back on your work efforts to a semi-retirement, or, express your desire to sell your company. In contrast to the way Bridget handled things, I believe it is best to be open with your management about your exit vision and to create some financial incentive for them to stay when the exit happens. This openness will actually inspire management to work toward achieving the exit strategy of the owner. Exiting owners can came up with incentives that keep management working toward the same goal and the same exit direction.

## KEY EXIT STRATEGY FACTORS TO CONSIDER

Whatever your dreams of business exit or retirement, this element is one factor every Personal Vision Statement should contain. But before you set a course that involves selling and leaving your business, consider and articulate the passion you have for your business and the impact that selling it one day will have on your personal happiness. Many owners have found that leaving their business behind had the effect of eliminating one of the most satisfying and fulfilling components of their lives. Look at other options. You may be happier keeping hold of your business, but restructuring it so you are able to spend less time at the office.

You can clarify your dreams for the future by considering the importance of such exit strategy factors as:

- **Selling or leaving the business to family**

- **Selling the business to outsiders**

- **Succession plans**

- **Retirement or semi-retirement**

## SELLING OR LEAVING BUSINESS TO FAMILY MEMBERS

A key question that must be answered by owners of family

businesses is, "Do I want my business to be kept in the family, or do I want to sell it to an outside party?" Another difficult challenge is deciding whether to sell or to gift the business to a family member or members, if you decide to keep it in the family. For some, the Personal Vision Statement expresses the wish to give ownership to some family members working in the business, but not to other family members who are also working in the business. If this is the case, there should be some strategy for handling any repercussions likely to happen with family members who will not be receiving ownership in the business. Many business owners have addressed this potential problem by balancing some non-business ownership factor, such as another type of economic benefit for the family member or members who are not receiving ownership.

For example, the founder of Conroy Technologies, Sam Conroy, employed his sons Doug and Mark Conroy for several years as Conroy Technologies' top two executives. However, Sam's third son showed no interest or aptitude in the family business. Sam expressed in his Personal Vision Statement his desire for his two sons employed in the business to own the business equally at the time of his death. When Sam died, the two brothers received equal ownership of the business. Sam Conroy provided for the third brother, by leaving him ownership of some commercial real estate he owned, and provided additionally for him with an insurance policy.

In family businesses, it is very common for the business owner to have a Personal Vision Statement of transitioning ownership to family members. In such cases, the business owner should clearly identify in their Personal Vision Statement which family members will have ownership in the company, and what percentage of ownership each shall have. The Personal Vision Statement should also clearly outline who among these family members will direct the business.

## WARNING! READ THIS BEFORE SELLING OR LEAVING EQUAL OWNERSHIP IN BUSINESS TO CHILDREN

If you are thinking about business ownership ultimately passing to family members with equal ownership, consider this carefully before you put it into your Personal Vision Statement. Equal ownership creates challenges, as no one party has the final say. Leaving a business equally to your children can be a formula for conflict. The specific roles of each family member need to be clearly defined.

## SELLING BUSINESS TO OUTSIDERS

If you plan to sell your business to an outside party, this strategy should be in your Personal Vision Statement. Bridget Baker had a long-term plan of selling Baker Manufacturing, which she expressed in her Personal Vision Statement. But she kept this desire as a Pocket Factor for fear that some managers would quit if they knew. Bridget's philosophy was that her vision of selling the business in 10 years was, "no one's business but my own." Many business owners feel that sharing their exit strategy could have a negative impact on the performance and/or retention of key executives, so they keep it to themselves. Bridget, at one point, made a decision that for her 10-year exit strategy to succeed, her business needed to get to the level where for at least three years it could show that the business generated profits of over $500,000 per year. She had received advice that this level of results was needed before she could expect to be able to sell the company at her desired minimum price. She shared her profit goal with her key executives, but kept in her "pocket," her vision to sell the business.

## SUCCESSION PLANS

Selecting and grooming your intended successor is an important part of preparing your company for sale. It cannot be left to fate, nor can it be done overnight. Depending on the age, ability and experience of your designated successor, this grooming period can take a long time to accomplish. As well, consider who will need to run the business during the transitioning time, if you were to become incapacitated or die and the business had to be put up for sale. During the sale period, the business needs to be run by someone, if you want to receive a fair price for the business. Likewise, if you intend to leave your business to someone, you need to prepare that person to run the business.

## SEMI OR COMPLETE RETIREMENT

The factor of semi or complete retirement is not one that many business owners under the age of 40 even want to consider when writing their Personal Vision Statement. But at some point in your life, you will consider this factor. The desire for retirement plays a significant role in eventual happiness, but this is a topic that most business owners view as taboo and put off until they are getting up in years. The reality is that many business owners never want to retire.

During a coaching session with Bridget's father, Sean Baker, who founded Baker Manufacturing, Sean told me, with obvious excitement about future projects he intended to work on. At the time of the session, Sean was in his mid 80s and still working part-time in the Baker Fabrication business. Sean had delegated most of his CEO responsibilities years earlier and had withdrawn/stepped back from the day-to-day business activities, but he was still spending time on specific projects that he enjoyed.

I asked him why he still worked so hard at his age, adding, "You are financially secure and don't need to work." He answered, "It's not about the money. I do it because I live it and love it. I go to bed at night thinking about my current and future projects and getting up in the morning with a purpose." Sean explained that he had considered full retirement at one point and even created a list of ways he might like to spend his free time upon retirement. The results of this simple exercise caused him to realize that he had no activities outside the business that brought him as much satisfaction as his involvement with his business. Sean's business clearly fulfilled him and he died while still involved – with his boots on, so to speak.

There was a time that our ancestors were so busy surviving against the elements and the need to fight off starvation that they didn't have the time to worry about things such as their "purpose" in life. Humans existing in today's world have had lives enriched with education, vacations and work weeks that aren't centered on finding food. This relative ease of living has also provided modern humankind with a great deal of time to consider whether our lives have meaning and purpose. Humans have a need for meaning in their life; it's one of the most important factors in a successful life. I believe that business owners, to a much greater extent than the average person, need a sense of purpose to feel satisfied. Many, who have become successful in business to a point where they have lost their purpose, suffer from depression and others have tried to escape their lives through alcohol and other drugs. Without a sense of purpose, which happens all too often when business owners sell their business, many of them, figuratively shrivel up and emotionally die.

If your vision is to semi or completely retire at a certain age, what do you want to do in retirement? A few years before his death, Sam Conroy, the owner of Conroy Technologies, expressed the following in his Personal Visions Statement: "Grow my business to a point where I can work less and have my two sons run the business day-to-day." We then discussed his plans for what he would be doing when he had increased time away from the business. His response was the same as I've heard a lot of business owners who push off the question by saying, "I'll develop hobbies after I retire."

While hobbies are great, claiming you'll find some down the road simply isn't good enough. If your vision is to semi-retire or completely retire at some point, include that vision in your Personal Vision Statement and define what you will do to fill the time you currently devote to work. Many business owners have retired only to find themselves lost, listless, unmotivated and miserable.

If you are considering semi-retirement, you need to consider how big your salary and/or dividends need to be from the business and whether the business can support you and the person who will be running the business day-to-day. You will need to make assumptions as to inflation, earnings growth on investments, and the tax rate your income will be taxed at upon retirement.

How much money will you need to retire so you can fulfill your envisioned and desired retirement lifestyle? Knowing this amount will help you determine the level of proceeds from the sale of your business needed to carry your projected lifestyle, or maybe you will need to stay on in a consulting role or other capacity in order to collect ongoing paychecks for some period of time.

If complete retirement is part of your dream for the future, you will want to include in your Personal Vision Statement the number of years leading up to your desired retirement. This time frame is needed so that you can make plans to be financially prepared, when the time comes, without your current income from your business.

**SHARING PERSONAL VISION STATEMENTS**

I mentioned earlier that I was once part owner and President of Tipton Centers, Inc., a retail consumer electronics chain that became a publicly traded company. For years, Sylvan Kaplan, my co-owner, and I both had a long-term vision of taking the company public. For years, we didn't share this long-term dream with our employees -- not even our top executives, our suppliers or customers. Sylvan and I kept this information tucked away "in our pockets" because we did not know if the vision was attainable, and also we didn't want our employees overwhelmed by the magnitude of our dream. Only after Tipton's sales and profit level gave us a reasonable chance at taking Tipton public did we take the dream out of our pockets and then shared the dream with certain key employees for Tipton to eventually become a listed, publically traded company. At a point in time when we felt confident that our "going public" dream was realistically attainable, we told this vision for Tipton's future to our top executives. During the years that we did not share this dream of going public, we always made sure our Company Vision Statement was consistent with our Personal Vision Statement.

## PUTTING IT ALL TOGETHER

Now, it's your turn. Use your desires relating to the Personal Vision Statement factors to write your Personal Vision Statement, using less than 100 words.

# COMPANY VISION STATEMENT

In this chapter you will learn the Blueprint process for developing your written Company Vision Statement. Your Company Vision Statement should answer the question, "What do I want the company to become, five to ten years from now?"

You, as the business owner, need to create the written Company Vision Statement because it will show your long-term expectations for the future you envision for your business. Your Company Vision Statement is the summit of your dreams for your company. It is the pinnacle destination that you want your company to reach. You must feel so passionate about the Company Vision Statement that you will be dedicated to making it happen.

By putting your vision for your company's future in writing and sharing this future with your employees, your employees will be focused on a set destination. As noted business author Ken Blanchard, stated, "Leadership is the act of arousing, engaging and satisfying the motives of followers in an environment of...change that results in the followers taking a course of action toward a mutually shared vision."

Your Company Vision Statement will help you to strategically lead your employees to the destination by inspiring commitment to the realization of your dream. Knowing the desired destination will help your employees make decisions and take actions, day in and day out, that lead towards your company vision for its future. With a clearly written Company Vision Statement in place, you and your employees are more likely to pick the straightest path to your destination, including goals, strategies, and action plans that will get you to your vision for the future of your company.

## COMPANY VISION STATEMENT MUST BE SYNERGISTIC WITH YOUR PERSONAL VISION STATEMENT

Your company is the power that propels you towards your Personal Vision of success and happiness. Your Personal and Company Vision Statements must be synergistic and in alignment with one another. Don Schlueter, a TAB-Certified Facilitator Coach in Chicago, Illinois, reflects that, "the only true business failures I've seen have been when the owner's Company Vision and Personal Vision were in conflict. There has to be a synergy between the two. The Personal Vision Statement of the business owner and the Company Vision Statement have to be working in tandem for the privately owned business to be truly successful."

If you are like most business owners, there are many other aspects of the business, in addition to the financial results, that will be factored into your Company Vision Statement. For example, company image or recognition may be just as important, if not more important to you than generating increased wealth.

While you may want to get advice from certain employees concerning how your Company Vision Statement is expressed, you, the business owner, are the only one qualified to determine the key factors that should be in your Company Vision Statement. This is because the purpose of your business is to satisfy your desires, not those of your employees. Sometimes this means saying no to employees who have different ideas about the future of your business.

During a meeting that was intended to finalize the Company Vision Statement for Baker Fabrication, Bridget Baker, her CFO and Operations VP suggested that the Baker Fabrication Company Vision Statement show a future that would include regional offices. The executives expressed to Bridget their belief that within a few years after the regional office expansion, Bridget would be able to take hundreds of thousands of dollars a year in distribution income. To their surprise, she was not excited about the regional expansion and did not include this expansion factor in the Company Vision Statement. During the meeting she explained to them that she was satisfied with the very low six-figure income that she was already making from the business. She explained that she felt that the company expansion would not be successful without her personal commitment and involvement, and that she did not want the out-of-town travel that would be required of her to personally stay on top of the new regional offices.

## COMPANY VISION STATEMENT SHOULD MOTIVATE EMPLOYEES

It may be your Company Vision, but if you have employees, you're going to need their help to make it happen. Leading your business strategically, requires that you take measures to ensure every employee is inspired to give their best on-the-job efforts directed at achieving your long-term dreams of company success.

For your Company Vision Statement to inspire employees, it must bring about more than a clear understanding by employees of the Company Vision that they are working towards. A good Company Vision Statement should keep your employees engaged and excited about the company's future. It should be grounded in reality, while creating a high level of challenge and stimulation.

Ideally, your Company Vision Statement should be written in a way that will motivate your employees to focus on activities that will help make your dreams for the future of the business happen. Your business is most likely to reach your vision if your business has the level of motivation that exists when every employee understands and is working towards the same "long view" dreams for the company. To bring about this level of motivation, your Company Vision Statement should resonate with all of your employees, creating pride and excitement about being part of something much bigger than themselves.

# COMPANY VISION STATEMENT:
# ADDITIONAL FACTORS TO CONSIDER

The following questions will help you think about our Company Vision Statement business factors and how you would like things to appear for the future of your company.

## PRINCIPAL PRODUCTS AND SERVICES FACTORS:

- What should your company's principal products/services look like in the immediate future? In five to ten years?

- What new products/services or business fields would you like to add?

- Which of your current products/services or business fields would you like to stop offering?

- What do you expect to be significantly different about your business products/services or market approach in the future?

- What quality standards do you need to meet?

## OPERATIONAL FACTORS

- What company operational activities do you want your company to be outstanding in?

- What level of productivity and performance do you want from your business?

## ECONOMIC FACTORS

- What economic or financial results are integral to achieving your company vision, such as operating on a sound financial basis or continuous profitable growth?

## CULTURAL AND VALUES FACTORS

- Why does your business exist beyond what it provides for you and your family? (E.g., a central belief at TAB is to provide life-changing services to the business owner community.)

- What principles, beliefs and values are essential to your vision of the company? (E.g., employee honesty and integrity that fosters an open, friendly and strategic workplace.)

- What social values are integral to your vision of the company? (E.g., contributing to the local community.)

- Do you want your company to budget for charitable contributions?

- Do you want your company to have a specific positive environmental impact?

## CUSTOMERS AND CLIENTS FACTORS

- Who would you like as your future customers, clients or users?

## HEADQUARTERS FACTORS

- Where do you want to locate your business's headquarters?

- Do you want to own or lease the property?

- In what geographical areas do you want to market?

- What other physical or virtual outlets/distribution channels would you like your company using in the future?

## COMPANY CULTURE FACTORS

- What is your management approach or philosophy?

- What is the philosophy for compensation and career growth opportunities for employees?

## COMPANY POSITION, IMAGE OR RECOGNITION FACTORS

- What company image do you seek in your industry? (E.g., to be seen as innovative)

- What level of leadership in your industry/professional services area/community do you want to have?

- What market share do you want? (E.g., being the biggest in revenue size or position locally, regionally, nationally or worldwide in your industry?)

## DON'T BE TOO WORDY

Prioritize the answers you have just written and write out the edited Company Vision Statement. A clear Company Vision Statement reflects your dreams of long-term company success and will allow your employees to be more likely to embrace your passion for the business themselves. Most business owners are so passionate about their business they find it difficult to not include everything they think is important in the Company Vision Statement. However, Company Vision Statements that are too wordy are less likely to be understood by employees. They will just ignore it.

Your first draft of the Company Vision Statement will probably be several hundred words. Your second draft needs to cut it down for what will be posted on your company office walls, your website, and so on. I had to do this with my first draft of TAB's Company Vision Statement. I began with the points listed below.

- To be the world's largest franchise system providing peer advisory and coaching solutions to business owners.

- To be agents of change who encourage and empower our members, based on real-world experience, to achieve their business and personal vision in every country where privately owned businesses are permitted to operate.

- To operate on a sound financial basis with steady profit growth.

- To be innovative without high risk.

- To have an open, friendly, and strategic management approach to leadership.

- To retain employees who work with a high level of productivity and a spirit of honesty, integrity, and teamwork.

- To have the best processes and protocols for our corporate staff and franchisees.

- To be headquartered in an office building that we own, located in the Denver, Colorado metropolitan area.

- To have a TAB brand that is identified with consistent quality and service with each TAB-Certified Facilitator Coach offering the same basic processes, systems, tools and quality.

- To have franchisees who are passionate about providing the highest level of facilitating and coaching services, who enjoy bringing about life-changing services to business owners, and who provide uniform value to business owners using our proprietary processes, products and services.

- To provide our franchisees with the needed continuing education and training for them to provide outstanding levels of facilitation and coaching.

After looking at the factors in my long-range dream for TAB, it was clear that I couldn't post a Company Vision Statement with several hundred words. I abstracted from the points. I first identified those things that I thought were essential in guiding our employees, facilitator/coaches, potential facilitator/coaches and members. This resulted in the following short and concise Company Vision Statement for TAB, which is strategically displayed at the entrance of our corporate offices, on our business cards and on our web site for all to see:

*"To be a leading international provider of peer advisory and coaching solutions to leaders of privately held businesses. Based on real-world experience, we will encourage and empower our members to achieve their Company and Personal Vision."*

## ARDEN CONSTRUCTION'S COMPANY VISION STATEMENT

Andrew Arden, our small company member, wanted to communicate to his clients and prospects a message that there was more to his business than mere profits. He wanted customers to understand that he truly cared about the services he provided. He wanted his Company Vision Statement to reflect his integrity. Andrew created a short, meaningful, and exciting Company Vision Statement to attract like-minded employees, clients and vendors. Andrew's full Company Vision Statement states:

Arden Construction is a leading provider of affordable, on-time high quality construction to those located within our metro area. We commit to:

- **Train our personnel so that they sell our services with honesty and knowledge.**

- **Use high quality materials that can be bought at reasonable prices.**

- **Employ a loyal workforce that is enlightened and passionate about the benefits of our services, and motivated to help customers receive those benefits.**

Some may feel that his Company Vision Statement is nothing more than a "mom and apple pie" cliché. But it works for Andrew because his clients and employees like it. He has posted the written Company Vision Statement in his office. To reinforce it, he has stitched into the employee uniforms the three adjectives that resonated with him most – "Affordable, On-Time, Quality Construction." Company vehicle signage also displays the phrase.

## FEEDBACK ON YOUR COMPANY VISION STATEMENT

Even if you own a smaller company, like Arden Construction, which does not have a staff of employees that you can go to for feedback, you should discuss your Company Vision Statement with your TAB Board members and your TAB-Certified Facilitator Coach to get their reactions and suggestions before posting it for your employees, customers and suppliers to see.

Your informal advisors will rarely have input that greatly changes the essence of your Company Vision Statement. They may challenge you on how realistic it is that your Company Vision will be accomplished. Often, they will provide suggestions for better ways to express your dream for the long-term future of your company. Expect suggestions to make your Company Vision Statement more motivating in language without changing the essence of what you, the business owner, want for the future of your company.

# 6

# CO-OWNERS

If there are co-owners of your business, it is essential that Personal Vision Statements by each of the co-owners be developed and shared among each of them, as it may affect the business. Each of you needs to identify how each wants to be living in the future and the relationship each wants with the business. If these Personal Vision Statements have any key factors in conflict with one another that may impact in any way on the business, these conflicts are resolved first, before creating a Company Vision, in order to create a unified destination for the efforts of the company.

One of the Personal Vision factors that must be shared is how much time each of the co-owners is willing to commit to working in the business. When creating Personal Vision Statements, we determine the balance we want to have between our business life and our non-business life. A CEO co-owner who wants to spend several weeks a year on vacation is going to need someone who can fulfill the CEO's responsibilities for him when he is away from the business. The amount of time a co-owner wants to devote to the business affects a lot of decisions such as how much high-level staffing the company needs.

At many TAB Board meetings that I have attended around the world, a co-owner has brought up the different views co-owners have on life/work balance. Many co-owners end up resentful about having the same compensation as another co-owner when their respective efforts and contributions to the company are different.

Shortly after the death of Sam Conroy and the passing of Conroy Technologies to Doug and Mark, I watched unpleasant and heated exchanges between Doug and Mark. Doug saw himself as the final decision maker for the software division of the business. However, Doug didn't want to grow the software division due to his growing responsibilities with the Rotary Club and his desire to retire five to 10 years in the future. Doug did not know that Mark had a desire to become the CEO of both divisions of Conroy Technologies and that Mark felt a driving passion for this type of work. Mark already considered himself the final decision maker of both divisions of the company and did not respect Doug's view of what the software division should be like long-term, or what their future roles within the business should be.

With some prompting by Mark's Facilitator/Coach, the brothers decided to share their Personal Vision Statements with each other. Remaining ignorant of this information would have opened the gates to a big problem with expansion dreams for the company. By discussing this factor, they were able to develop a minimum level of compatibility between these dreams that resulted in a written Company Vision Statement they could both support relating to expansion and to Mark's desire for a greater role in the company. Sharing written Personal Vision Statements is indispensible in getting co-owners on the same page. Left unaddressed, a lack of alignment on Personal Visions will have an impact on the results of the company and the plans needed to achieve different long-term results.

## COMPANY VISION STATEMENTS OF MULTIPLE OWNERS

Co-owners' key factors for the vision for the company must be in alignment for the owners to work synergistically together and lead their business forward. These factors can significantly affect company decisions such as how aggressively to expand the business, or whether to expand at all. All co-owners should identify their long-term work role desires for what they want to be doing in the business. All too often, one of the co-owners has an idea of what the other co-owner should be doing in the business, but that is not what that other co-owner wants. They need to discuss their passions.

If the written Company Vision Statement is not compatible with any key factors in the Personal Vision Statement of one of the co-owners, it is likely the business will underperform because it doesn't have full support at the top level for the same strategic direction. Getting alignment on the Company Vision Statement may cause a delay in finalizing it, but it is worth it if the extra time results in a Company Vision Statement that meets the basic needs of all the co-owners for the long-term future of the business.

If there are multiple owners of the business, all the owners and their employees should work towards the Company Vision Statement.

Without alignment on the Company Vision Statement, you risk the chance that co-owners will work against each other, sometimes intentionally. Each may be harnessing the efforts of employees to achieve a dream for the business that is theirs, but not the desires of other owners of the company. Different departments may follow desires of different owners who have different destinations for the business. To create an aligned Company Vision for a business with multiple owners, it's often helpful for the owners to meet with an outside facilitator, like a TAB-Certified Facilitator Coach, to resolve any areas of non-alignment in their wishes for the future of the company.

At the time the first Company Vision Statement was written for Conroy Technologies, the brothers, who co-owned the business, shared the desire for their company to expand to a minimum of three new major cities in the USA within the next 10 years. When this long-term expansion desire was discussed with Conroy's CFO, he explained that any banks willing to make the expansion loans and leases would require Doug to personally guarantee the loans.

Doug explained that part of his Personal Vision was not personally guaranteeing company loans or leases relating to the expansion because, "I plan on retiring in the next five to 10 years and don't want to guarantee any loans or leases that will endure after I retire." Consequently, the brothers agreed to a less aggressive expansion that could be done out of company generated cash flow. The Company Vision Statement contained a reference to operating offices in additional cities, without any specific minimum number of cities.

At Conroy Technologies, gaining the buy-in of both brothers on the Company Vision Statement that was shared with employees had a profound positive impact on the success of the business. Without such an alignment of the co-owners to the Company Vision Statement, one may be rowing their oars in a different direction than the others. It is easy to see how this can be counterproductive.

Resolving differences as to what the Company Vision Statement should look like starts with establishing an understanding of each other's dreams for the company. The best way of resolving these differences is to involve an impartial facilitator, such as a TAB-Certified Facilitator Coach. In these meetings, the co-owners can explore ways in which the company can meet the dreams of all the co-owners. When co-owners have trouble creating a Company Vision Statement that is mutually acceptable to all of them, negotiation among the co-owners typically ensues. The challenge to the Facilitator/Coach of such meetings is to keep the situation as unemotional as possible and focus the conversation solely on the facts that support each side's positions.

All owners should be involved in giving feedback and input on the Company Vision Statements, even if they have a small minority interest in the company. Their input can enrich the quality of the Company statements in a very special way since they have a vested interest that goes beyond that of most other employees. This need to be involved in giving feedback for the creation of the statements is particularly important for family members with ownership.

# THE BLUEPRINT BICYCLE

## THE BLUEPRINT BICYCLE OVERVIEW

Using the analogy of a bicycle, envision a Blueprint Bike that will help you "ride" toward your Personal Vision of long-term success. The objective of riding your Blueprint Bicycle is to get you to your Personal Vision of success. The Blueprint Front Wheel directs you to the destination of where you want to get to, which is your Personal Vision Statement. The Rear Wheel of your Blueprint Bike is the success of your business, which powers you towards your destination, your dreams of long-term success. You, as a business owner, are the rider of your Blueprint Bike. You will strategically steer your Blueprint Bike so that it does not go into a dead-end track, avoids detours that deter you from reaching your desired destination, keeps you from getting stuck off the path in bad terrain, and avoids the potholes on the trip.

DESTINATION POWER

## THE BLUEPRINT FRONT WHEEL: THE DESTINATION
## OF YOUR PERSONAL DREAMS OF SUCCESS

In the Blueprint process, your Personal Vision Statement, which is also the Front Wheel of the Blueprint Bicycle, identifies the kind of future you want to be living five to 10 years down the road. It sets the destination so you can map out the best way to get there. Your Company Vision must help power you to a Personal Vision, while being in sync with your dreams for the life you want to be living. Having only a vague vision of what you want for your future can cause your bicycle to wander off course and lead you seriously astray from reaching your dreams. Blueprint requires written documentation – a well thought-out statement of your desired long-term dreams for your personal destination. So, before putting your business wheel in motion by pedaling, creating the power from your business success, it is best to have a clear destination expressed in writing, which we've defined as your Personal Vision Statement.

## THE BLUEPRINT REAR WHEEL: YOUR BUSINESS SUPPLIES
## THE POWER TO REACH YOUR PERSONAL DREAMS

Your success in getting to your Blueprint Front Wheel destination--just like with any bike--is dependent on the power supplied by your Blueprint Rear Wheel. As a business owner, your Blueprint Rear Wheel power is the business success of your company that is so essential in bringing about your personal dreams. As you lead your business using Business Builder's Blueprint, you are pedaling your Blueprint Bike, with your efforts turning the Blueprint Rear Wheel that creates the power, or the business success, that takes you to the destination of your Blueprint Front Wheel – your Personal Vision Statement.

Your Company Vision Statement contains the aspirations you have for your company, as you want it to exist in the future. The Company Vision Statement of long-term business success must be compatible and synergistic with your long-term personal dreams to supply the power you need to attain your Personal Vision Statement when your company success takes place.

## TURNING YOUR BLUEPRINT BIKE WHEELS

Your Vision Statements are living statements. You many encounter certain specific impactful events that will require you to rethink and redefine your Personal and Company Vision Statements. Events may show that your Personal and Company Vision Statements are no longer realistic. Your Blueprint Bicycle wheels will keep turning and moving your company toward the direction of your Personal Vision Statement, but at times, you will need to rethink both of your Vision Statements.

In Blueprint we refer to this rethinking and possible revision of your Personal and Company Vision Statements as "Turning the Wheels."

Like your annual bicycle checkup, every part of your Blueprint Bike should be examined and tuned as this process reflects both your Front Wheel Personal Vision and your Rear Wheel Company Vision. Set aside time annually to review your Personal and Company Vision Statements for needed revisions due to your changed circumstances. This review involves looking at whether your Company Vision Statement is efficiently moving you towards and supplying the power needed to reach your Personal Vision Statement. To ride your Blueprint Bike to the destination of your dreams, the wheels need to be turning efficiently and require annual, thorough tune-ups during which you consider changed circumstances that have occurred since you wrote your Vision Statements.

Your Personal and Company Vision Statements should remain relatively constant unless a major change takes place in your life or business. An unexpected change of circumstances, such as health issues, family entering the business, birth of a child, divorce, or death of a loved one could require a significant change in written Personal and Company Vision Statements. At times there may be unexpected changes of circumstances that are so significant that your Vision Statements need to be reviewed right away. Even without any major changes, it is always a good idea to periodically review your Personal and Company Vision Statements to make sure they are still meaningful to you. Periodically reviewing these Vision Statements will also help reinforce your focus on the desired destination. Unless there is a significant change in personal circumstance, periodic "Turning the Wheels" reviews relating to your Personal

Vision Statement should take only a few minutes. But, if there is a change of circumstance relating to your Personal Vision Statement, considerable time will be required in order to rethink what you want in your personal long-term future.

Although your Company Vision Statement is also not likely to change very often, just reading it periodically will also help you stay focused on your desired destination for your company. Your Company Vision Statement helps you and your employees avoid losing sight of your long range target, which is easy to happen with the multitude of day-to-day things that fight for your attention. Any changes made to your Company Vision Statement should be considered carefully. Your Company Vision Statement is not to be trifled with by making spontaneous or frequent changes, as these changes may confuse your employees. But there are times changes are needed. When you do decide to change your Company Vision Statement, it will cause a ripple effect on other company statements that will also need to be addressed.

During the economic crisis that started in 2007, Arden Construction's Company Vision Statement changed to eliminating Andrew Arden's dreams to operate within a 300-mile region. That economic crisis hurt the construction industry severely, generally speaking. The business assessed this during its annual "Turning the Wheels" retreat. In 2009, Andrew Arden had two heart attacks in a short time period. Andrew had successfully run Arden Construction single-handedly for many years, and after his two heart attacks, he grew concerned about his possible impairment. His memory was slower than it had been, his physical strength was compromised, and, for the first time in his life, he found himself seeking help to develop an exit strategy rather than building his business as part of his dream. A revision of his Personal Vision Statement and Company Vision Statement was needed.

When Bridget Baker found out she was going to be a grandmother, she changed several Blueprint Statements. This is an example of a change in personal circumstance that resulted in Bridget reconsidering her Personal Vision Statements during monthly coaching sessions when she did a "Turning the Wheels" review.

Doug Conroy realized that he was experiencing burnout and dreading going to work. He didn't want to work the long hours, nor did he enjoy the day-to-day things he was doing at Conroy Technologies.

In each of these examples, Andrew Arden, Bridget Baker and Doug Conroy changed their Personal Vision Statements. For some business owners, their views about family, charitable efforts, hobbies, or even spiritual pursuits may take on a greater importance in their life than their business, due to life events that required them to revisit and modify their long-term dreams of success as expressed in their original Personal Vision Statement.

# ELEMENT 1:
# CONCLUSION

Business Builder's Blueprint is a journey with the end being to achieve your personal dreams. As with any journey, there are bound to be rough spots and even unexpected detours in reaching your dreams. Your long-term Personal Vision of success should have some level of balance between your business and non-business life. If not, you may find yourself among those business owners who sacrifice their personal lives to get their business to a level of success, only to find that the business's success has left them unfulfilled and personally miserable. Your unique Personal Vision needs to be a destination that will bring you business and personal fulfillment. Your dreams for your long-term future should include more than the material level of success that your business can bring you. Your Personal Vision Statement will address such things as: What are the functions you want to be doing at work? What are the intellectual and creative challenges at work that you need to keep your mind stimulated and excited about your business? Who are the people you want to spend time with at work? Are factors such as prestige and image important to you? Perhaps you would like more time away from the business during the week to spend with your family or hobbies. Or, perhaps you want more weeks a year away from business to relax and rejuvenate on vacation.

The reality is that for most business owners, your company results will provide the income, type of work, personal pride, image and other factors that are so important to their personal success. You have dreams for your company, such as the size of your company, and you should never stop focusing on the big dreams you want your company. You, as business owner, are the catalyst for strategically leading your company to the long-term success that is so important for the long-term dreams of most business owners. It's your business. You are at the controls, and control the destination of your company.

As I mentioned earlier, each of the four elements of Business Builder's Blueprint can be done without involving the other factors. Although it is preferable that you start your Blueprint efforts by first creating written Personal and Company Vision Statements, many TAB members have started Blueprint by first focusing on plans to help with their company's Critical Success Factor (CSFs). Regardless as to where in the Blueprint process a business owner starts, most do eventually create their written Personal Vision Statement and Company Vision Statement.

My sincere hope is that you will use Business Builder's Blueprint to realize your Personal and Company Visions of success, just as this valuable process has done for the thousands of TAB business owner members worldwide who are using Blueprint.

# ELEMENT 2:
# THE LOOK IN THE
# COMPANY MIRROR
# INTRODUCTION

In Element 1, I discussed the development of the business owner's Personal Vision Statement and Company Vision Statement, which collectively makes up the Element 1 of the Business Builder's Blueprint process. This element focuses on the evaluation of your business.

By nature, business owners want to go into action right away. Too often, they start taking action without standing back, taking in the landscape, and only then determining what the best strategic decision is in order to have the greatest chance of success. Only after the best strategic decision is made should plans be developed.

I believe in the expression, "Don't move the fence until you know what it's there for, and when you do move the fence, know when and where you need to move it." When you meet with a challenging business situation, you must be very strategic and avoid knee jerk reactions.

Business Builder's Blueprint bypasses the "hit-or-miss" approach to planning used by most business owners. Blueprint helps business owners organize and focus on each and every event to be dealt with in the ever-changing world of business. Blueprint takes the mystery out of what is involved in strategically leading a privately owned business. The process integrates the reality that most business owners need to both strategically lead and manage your company. Blueprint is built on the practical reality that business owners will also often be involved tactically at every level of the company.

Business owners using Blueprint no longer have to stress over those unknown curve balls that are thrown at them in the business world. When Blueprint is used for making decisions in your business, you know that you are, at last, in control of your company and its destiny.

## BLUEPRINT'S PROVEN BENEFITS

By using the Blueprint strategic planning process, you will be taking the single most important step to reach your company's full potential. The easy-to-use Blueprint strategic planning process is a tested and proven leadership process that has, for decades, helped business owners around the world achieve greater company profits and increase the value of their businesses.

By using the planning process that is so important to Blueprint, you will gain a collective commitment from your employees on company-critical success factors, goals, strategies and action plans. This will take place because your employees will share the same clear and easy-to-understand picture of the strategic direction you wish to take your company and the actions needed to get there.

The Blueprint strategic planning process will help your managers make the right decisions in regards to resources, time allocation, and effort for themselves and their subordinates. Lower priority issues will be reduced, and will increase the accountability that comes from a disciplined follow-up mechanism in which action plan results are reviewed against projected results, and modified as needed to maximize outcomes.

## ADAPT BLUEPRINT PLANNING FOR YOUR SIZE COMPANY

The business-planning element of Blueprint works for privately owned companies of all sizes. Blueprint is simple to customize for your particular size company. There is no privately owned business that is too small or too big to benefit from Blueprint. Element 2 will show you how to best utilize those elements of Blueprint that work for the unique challenges you bring to the strategic planning table, regardless of the limitations created by the size of your business. Companies with fewer than five employees use Blueprint, as well as those with multiple divisions or subsidiaries with independent profit and loss responsibilities who have found it just as easy to utilize Blueprint with one division or with each subsidiary having its own set of Blueprint Company Plans.

As well, Blueprint leadership techniques, processes and methods can be customized to best fit the management makeup and size of your company. Regardless of the size of your company, Blueprint must first be embraced by you, the business owner. In Element 2, I will show you how to adapt the techniques, processes and methods to your size company, which in this book, are referred to as Small-size, Mid-size and Large-size Companies.

## WRITTEN STATEMENTS

Each of your company preplanning steps and your actual Blueprint Company Plans require written statements, consisting of a series of clear and articulated bullet points, with individual written statements not exceeding 100 words, except for Tactics. Tactics may be unlimited and collectively are essential to the Action Plan being executed.

Get the perspective of both your management and your non-management employees' best "out-of-the-box" creative thinking as they relate to improving these Blueprint Company pre-planning and planning statements. For those of you who are TAB Board members, your TAB Board members and your TAB-Certified Facilitator Coach will be additional resources for challenging and advising you on your formal written Blueprint Company pre-planning and plan statements.

# A LOOK IN THE COMPANY MIRROR OVERVIEW:
# PRE-PLANNING STEP

The first step of the pre-planning stage, which needs to take place before your strategic planning, is an evaluation. We refer to this step as a "Look in the Company Mirror". Your "Look in the Company Mirror" consists of creating separate written statements assessing:

- **Your company's strengths**

- **Your company's weaknesses**

- **Your company's opportunities**

- **Your company's threats**

In Element 1, we discussed the importance of creating written Personal and Company Vision Statements. Hopefully, you now know what your dream is for the future of your company. Now is the time to do an evaluation of whether your dream is realistically attainable, and to set in motion the plans to attain your dreams for the long-term success of your company.

A "Look in the Company Mirror" requires a very objective and honest look at your company's Strengths, Weaknesses, Opportunities and Threats (SWOTs). These four factors are collectively referred to as your Company SWOT. Without doing SWOT evaluations, you will not know whether the factors in your Company Vision Statement are achievable, or what plans your company needs to develop in order to have a realistic possibility of achieving your long-term dreams for your Company.

This chapter will provide an overview of each of these four SWOT factors. The subsequent chapters in Element 2 will show you how to develop company statements for each SWOT factor. It is common for Company Vision Statement drafts to be revised after seeing the reality of a company. Also, since the business supplies the power for the business owner's Personal Vision Statement, it is common for this in turn to also bring about changes in the business owner's Personal Vision Statement.

The SWOT evaluation helps in creating realistic, strategically-focused company plans that best utilize your company strengths, neutralize any weaknesses, take advantage of opportunities and react to threats outside your control.

You, as the business owner, should create a draft of each of your Company SWOT Statements. Let your thoughts flow and jot down what comes to mind. This isn't the time to be a stickler for grammar and syntax. There will be ample opportunity for you to edit when you refine the drafts into formally written SWOT Statements, after verifying SWOT statements with survey data and other empirical evidence.

Creating SWOT Statements is easier than ever because of today's technology. Incredible amounts of information are available on the Internet, and data gathering tools like online surveys give unparalleled access to help you develop your SWOT Statements. Web-based surveys are effective and inexpensive ways to find out what your employees, customers and suppliers think about your company's Strengths, Weaknesses, Opportunities and Threats. Even small companies, such as Andrew Arden's, can develop and conduct such surveys. These surveys will help you evaluate and confirm the accuracy of your Company SWOT Statements.

## STRENGTHS (S)

The process of identifying your Company Strengths Statement is usually enjoyable because this statement contains the "good stuff." Company Strengths are the easiest company factors to leverage when trying to gain improved company results. These strengths are easy to identify because most of us know the areas in which our company excels.

You, the business owner, bring your business-related strengths to your company. In a small private company, your business skills are likely to be essential to the success of the business. The larger your business, the less your business is dependent on your specific business skills. However, regardless of the size of your business, your business should take advantage of your business-related strengths to the greatest extent possible.

## WEAKNESSES (W)

*"Recognizing a problem doesn't always bring a solution, but until we recognize that problem, there can be no solution." — James Baldwin*

It would be nice to reach the pinnacle of our dreams for your businesses and never come face-to-face with your company Weaknesses. But this isn't realistic if you want your company to achieve its greatest potential. Looking at your company's Weaknesses isn't always a "cake walk," and you may not like seeing the realities of the Weaknesses that have been causing your company to underachieve, compared to its potential. These Weaknesses are the critical shortcomings of your company that can keep you from reaching your Company Vision. You can't neutralize a Weakness without first identifying it, so you must honestly identify what you actually see in the mirror, not what you wish to see.

Your Company Weaknesses evaluation identifies weaknesses relating to both the business owner's personal business skills and to other weaknesses of the company. Write them down! Seeing these Weaknesses in writing will create an awareness that you may not have previously seen, and this is critically important.

Identifying your Company Weaknesses is like finding defective parts on your bike before you take your ride; you make the repairs or replace the parts so that your bike runs well, does not break down, or leave you stranded on the road to success. Business owners who fail to consider their Company Weaknesses find their Company Bicycle breaking down before they reach their desired destination.

With the kind of clarity that comes from a "Look in the Mirror" at your company Weaknesses, your Bike won't break down because of surprises caused from not paying attention.

## OPPORTUNITIES (O)

Identifying realistically attainable Opportunities that may add to the success for your company is usually exciting and stimulating! Each Opportunity that you list in your Company Opportunity Statement must lead toward your Personal and/or Company Vision Statements and if it doesn't, you should pass on the opportunity, regardless of how exciting it appears to be. Andrew Arden, our small private company owner, saw the opportunity to get a government contract that would have required him to double the size of his staff to fulfill the construction contract. He passed on the opportunity because the opportunity was in conflict with his Personal and Company's Vision Statement relating to the company's desired growth rate. Without his Blueprint plan, Andrew admitted his previous tendency would have been to jump on the opportunity without regard to its fit with his or the company's long-term needs.

Not all Opportunities are created equal. Just because a new opportunity exists doesn't necessarily mean you should go for it. Consider how an opportunity will affect company human and financial resource bandwidth. No company has the infrastructure and capital to tackle and achieve every opportunity. You determine if the opportunity is worth diverting your company from its current Company Plans. Consider whether the opportunity achieves your Company or Personal Vision Statements better than the

Opportunities where your company is currently focused.

Think twice about jumping on an opportunity just because it excites you or may be unbearably tantalizing. Most successful leaders have at some time taken assertive moves to advance their companies by grabbing hold of Opportunities with bold actions that require calculated risks. This is different than gambling. Some "blue sky" Opportunities, which sound great, are just not realistically attainable or practical.

Sometimes the opportunity that presents itself isn't right because you lack the proper amount time to follow through with a plan to take advantage of the opportunity. For example, creating a plan to take advantage of a new opportunity might require adding new employees or training current employees on new skills to take advantage of the opportunity at a time that your company is not in a position to shift resources that are currently needed elsewhere.

## THREATS (T)

> "Don't be afraid of opposition. Remember, a kite rises against—not with—the wind." –Hamilton Mabie (American essayist, d. 1916)

Identifying Threats to a company is, for many business owners, a very fearful and stressful experience. Unlike the excitement that often takes place when company Opportunities are considered, looking at threats to your business can be anything but exciting because Threats your company is facing today (and which you may face tomorrow) can have a significantly negative impact. To prevent the negative impact, as Jack Welch, former President of General Electric said, you must "Face reality as it is, not as it was or as you wish it to be."

Just as some miss the window for eliminating or neutralizing a health problem by not taking the steps for early detection, you might also miss out on a chance to proactively protect your business from a threat that could hurt your company's long-term health. Putting off the examination of the situation could be the most detrimental non-action a business could encounter. Writing your Company Threats Statement is the key to early detection.

The type of Threats I am referring to include those that are outside your control. For example, you have no control over whether there is a global recession, advancements in technology by competitors, changes in social consciousness of the nation. Other factors can turn a formerly non-existent or benign factor into a looming threat. New Threats to your company can appear at any time. Typewriter manufacturers were once incredibly successful, and then were rapidly eliminated by the computer. Kodak, which once dominated the film development business, suffered greatly when digital cameras became the dominant mode of photography. Many manufacturers that long depended on non-recyclable packaging did not visualize or adjust to the impact from green-thinking buyers.

But even though you can't stop these types of Threats from happening, you can – most of the time – minimize their effect. Writing out your Threats Statement will help your company focus on developing proactive measures to protect your company. After you recognize significant Threats to your company, you will want to develop armor to protect against such Threats. This armor may, at times, involve significant changes in the course that your company is traveling, while at the same time sidestepping anything that might break apart or destroy what is working for your company. Sometimes Threats require reevaluation and modification of your current business model.

Creating your Company Threats Statement is the first step in showing the need to develop a company response that can bypass serious potholes in its travels. Once you identify a major threat to your company in your Statement, you are able to develop Company Plans that may prevent or minimize a serious problem for your company. You want to have the maximum amount of time to prepare your company to leap these hurdles if and when they appear. Early awareness of Threats, followed by the development of Company Plans has meant, for many business owners, the difference between saving and losing their businesses.

Let's now look at each of these SWOT factors in greater depth and I will show you the type of thinking that will help you identify each of the SWOT statements for your company. In each of your company SWOT statements, it is important to look at what impact you, as the business owner, bring to the SWOT factors in your company, as well as all the many other business factors that are important to the overall evaluation of your business.

# COMPANY STRENGTHS

## COMPANY STRENGTHS RELATING TO THE BUSINESS OWNER

Andrew Arden, owner of Arden Construction, expressed his Company Strength as: "The owner's knowledge of quality construction methods." The degree of importance that your strength means to your company usually varies with the stage of your company's development. At the start-up or early stage of a business such as Arden Construction's, the dependence on the Personal Business Strengths of the founder/business owner is usually greater. In many cases, during the start-up or early stage, these Personal Business Strengths of the owner are the primary Strengths of the company. As more employees join your company, there is typically less dependence on the owner's Personal Business Strengths, and it is less likely that your company will need to ride the "coattails" of the owner's Personal Business Strengths.

As the owner, you want to make maximum use of your Personal Business Strengths to increase your impact on the success of your company. The better use you make of your Strengths, the more effectively you will be a powerful engine to propel your movement toward the dreams set forth in your Personal Vision Statement.

To identify your Personal Business Strengths, write down those major activities that you spend much of your time doing at your business. For example, if you analyze company financial statements, then hopefully, this is one of your strength areas.

Next, ask yourself whether you have a driving passion to do the work activity you just identified. Every business owner I know who has a greatly successful company shares in common that they personally have an obsessive focus with certain activities at work that are greatly important to the success of the company. Their obsessive passion drives them to focus in a way that brings about leaps of creative improvement for their companies.

Passion for areas of work that you do in your company is first and foremost in identifying your Personal Business Strengths. Without this passion for specific activities, you can be excellent at the activities, but probably will not give them your best long-term effort. Certainly, engaging in activities you lack passion for will bring about less enjoyment at work.

If you have passion for a particular business activity, you may become obsessively focused on excelling in that activity. This creates exceptional focus on getting results that simply would not happen without the passion.

Generally speaking, people only feel passionate about doing activities that match their natural personality or, as others refer to it, their natural behavioral style. Your passion is essentially who you are. There are many personality and behavioral style assessments that inexpensively provide analysis of your basic nature. You don't have to adapt or force yourself to do the activities you love. If the activity seems contrary to your natural personality/behavioral style, this will undoubtedly create stress in your life. If business activities are in harmony with you basic personality/behavioral style, you will enjoy the experience. Bottom line: you need to do "what you are" to best support your long-term efforts.

The flip of this coin is that passion alone is not enough. Passion without aptitude is not enough to put these activities among your Personal Business Strengths.

Before listing your Personal Business Strengths in your Company Strengths Statement, ask whether these strengths have the potential to make a major positive impact on your company ("Big Picture Potential"). Just because you have a Personal Business Strength doesn't mean that it is something that is worth listing on your Company Strengths Statement. List only those Personal Business Strengths you have that have Big Picture Potential to the company.

Now, the reality is that the smaller the business, the more likely it is that you may have to spend a great deal of time doing things you don't enjoy, and which may not have Big Picture Potential. If the activities that you spend much of time doing at work do not have Big Picture Potential, you should give serious thought to how you can transition your efforts at work toward more Big Picture Potential responsibilities.

When Bridget, who owns Baker Manufacturing, identified the activities where she spends most of her time, she pointed out how much passion she had for interacting with prospects and using her strong selling skills to persuade them to do business with her company. Baker Manufacturing is our mid-sized private company example, and Bridget has focused her energy and passion on increasing revenues. Her ability to open an increasing number of new major accounts has Big Picture Potential to bring about a major increase in company sales. Her Company Strengths Statement reflects her Personal Business Strength as follows:

- **Creates, develops and maintains strong relationships with key account customers.**

This Personal Business Strength would be used later in a Company Plan that involved increasing her time spent on selling big accounts, which in turn, helped her company achieve its Company Vision.

## COMPANY STRENGTHS OTHER THAN PERSONAL BUSINESS STRENGTHS OF OWNERS

Once you have identified your Personal Business Strengths, it's time to do the same for the other Company Business Strengths. The Business Builder's Blueprint process prompts your thinking with questions. Bridget identified her company Strengths by answering the same type of questions below that you will need to answer as they relate to your business. The questions are not intended to be all encompassing and, in fact, some of the questions may not apply at all to your business.

## MANAGEMENT AND OTHER PERSONNEL

- **What departments or members of your management**

team have a demonstrated outstanding ability that can best contribute to building the value of your business? Consider competencies such as strategic thinking, innovative thinking, technological savvy, team building acumen, customer relations skills, innovative use of resources, communication skills, problem solving, mentoring ability, great leadership skills, and any other Strengths that your leadership team members and/or departments bring to the table.

- Do management team members have a high level of business experience?

- Does your company have a belief system or company culture that leads to a more effective or competitive organization?

## FINANCIAL FACTORS

- What prevailing financial factors may have the greatest positive influence on your company, such as having no outstanding debt?

- What patents or other intellectual property and/or trademarked services are owned by your company?

- Does your company have a financial risk-taking philosophy that could be viewed as a Company Strength?

## SALES AND MARKETING

- Does your sales department excel at selling company products/services using an effective sales system?

- What aspect of your marketing is the most effective in getting sales leads?

## MANUFACTURING, OPERATIONS AND DISTRIBUTION

- Does your company have a low-cost manufacturing process? If so, what benefits are gained from it?

- Does your company have up-to-date and efficient information systems?

- Is your company certified by the International Organization for Standardization (ISO)?

- What are your company's strongest and most effective outlets/distribution channels?

- List any miscellaneous factors that give your company an outstanding edge, such as a retail location for your company that offers you a competitive advantage.

## PRODUCTS/SERVICES

- How are your products/services more beneficial or value-added compared to competitors?

- How is your company innovative?

You may come up with questions on your own that were not included here. Stimulate your evaluative thinking!

Hopefully, writing down the answers to these questions will help you write the first draft of your Company Strengths Statement. Once you have answered relevant questions, go back and take a second look at what you have written. Make sure you are satisfied that your answers clearly represent your current Company Strengths.

Your Company Strengths have different degrees of potential to impact your company. Take the time to choose which Strengths have the potential to have the biggest impact in your company's ability to reach the future you desire. Your formal written Company Strengths Statement should only contain the Personal Business Strengths and other Company Strengths that have the most potential for leverage.

When you're done, finalize the Strengths to no more than five. Limit the final Company Strengths Statement to 100 words or less.

Bridget identified the Strengths of her manufacturing business, other than her Personal Business Strengths, as the following:

- Experienced management and manufacturing personnel

- Since 2001 have had a well-documented manufacturing process and systems

- Patents on certain products and parts

- The manufacturing plant is solely owned by Bridget, which eliminates concern about increased rent in the future

- The manufacturing plant has room for a great amount of expansion.

## START WRITING YOUR COMPANY STRENGTHS STATEMENT

Once you have answered the applicable Company Strength evaluation questions, consider the importance of each of your answers. Your Company Strengths have different degrees of potential positive impact for your company to reach the future you desire. Make sure your Company Strengths Statement is limited to those that have the biggest upside potential to help attain the Company Vision.

Now that we've looked at Company Strengths, we're ready to look at Company Weaknesses.

CHAPTER 10

# COMPANY WEAKNESSES

## COMPANY WEAKNESSES RELATING TO THE BUSINESS OWNER

Very often, the greatest company Weakness relates to an over-dependence on the business owner. Andrew Arden stated that the greatest Weakness of his company was, "Dependence on me for generating all new business."

Sometimes the greatest Weakness of the company ties in with a personal Weakness of the business owner. Mark Conroy, owner of our large private company, had a dream of doubling the size of his technology consulting division within five years, but it didn't happen. The problem that stood in the way was Mark's inability to strategically lead his company. When Mark joined TAB and committed to using Blueprint, I met with Kevin, Mark's Executive Vice President. During this meeting with Kevin, with the approval of Mark, Kevin mentioned that it was no surprise to him that the growth plans for the company were not met. Kevin expressed his belief that the failure of the company to grow was because Mark got easily caught up in handling day-to-day matters.

He explained his view that Mark's brilliance with technological innovation did not translate well into Mark being as an effective leader. Kevin talked about how tough things were on a typical day for him and other executives because of Mark's very spur-of-the-moment involvement in day-to-day matters, without any strategic direction. I asked Kevin if he had ever approached Mark about the problem. "Oh, I've tried," Kevin sighed, "but Mark doesn't really see the truth of how ineffectively he operates."

When talking to Mark during our coaching session to create his first draft of a Company Weaknesses Statement, he listed his following Personal Business Weaknesses:

- **Very much overweight, which hinders my peak performance**

- **Involved in too many political and/or social activities, which takes away time from my business**

- **Lack of self accountability**

- **Weak at strategic leadership, financing, marketing, and sales**

He stated that each of these Personal Business Weaknesses affected his contribution to his business. I discussed his reference to being weak at strategic leadership and opened up the discussion about his tendency to over focus on day-to-day matters. Mark expressed that while he was really good at technological innovation and solving specific project problems, he was weak at the process involved for strong strategic planning. We were able to get out in the open that Mark's focus on day-to-day matters versus strategic planning was a significant company Weakness that could be hurting his company's growth to the next level.

Mark, not surprisingly, did not feel comfortable including the Personal Business Weaknesses concerning his weight, the diversion of his time to outside activities, or the lack of self accountability in the draft Company Weaknesses Statement that employees and management were to see. Because he didn't feel comfortable sharing these Personal Business Weaknesses, he wrote these down as Pocket Personal Business Weaknesses. He later created a personal plan to do something about each of these Weaknesses. Only you, as the company owner, can decide which of your Personal Business Weaknesses you are willing to share with some or all of your employees.

Mark shared, in his Company Weaknesses Statement that "I get too caught up in handling day-to-day matters." A result of identifying this weakness was a Company Plan trying to neutralize Mark's Personal Business Weakness.

When I was part-owner and Chief Operating Officer at Tipton, I allowed a Personal Business Weakness to interfere with my judgment. I became social friends with one of my executives. This friendship reached a point where my wife and I, the executive, and his wife took vacations together. The executive was a very bright man, and I enjoyed his company. At one point, he experienced some personal problems. He wasn't showing up to work on time in the morning. Other executives began to complain to me about this.

How did I handle it? I defended him by explaining that the executive was going through a problem period and hopefully it would be resolved soon. I was the source of the Company Weakness in this situation because I made excuses for him that I would have not have made for any other employee. This double standard caused problems. You cannot allow even the appearance of a protected class of employee. If you do, you will create a cultural Weakness in your company that will lead to resentful employees. If you do develop a social relationship with one of your employees, you cannot give this employee any special treatment or even allow the appearance of a protected class. The following are some of the questions that will help you identify those of your Personal Business Weaknesses that may have "Big Picture" negative impact on your business:

- **What tasks or responsibilities do you not enjoy doing; possibly dread doing for any reason? Include things for which you may not have the natural ability/aptitude needed to excel, or that go against your natural personality/behavioral style. Where must you adapt your style to in order to get those jobs done? This might be a clue! (E.g., selling your company products or services, developing operational protocols, handling employee conflict, firing employees, conducting employee reviews.)**

- Have you created a personal/social relationship with an employee that is causing resentment from other employees or accountability problems? (Suppliers and vendors may also fall into this category.)

- Is your company too dependent on you? (You are a slave to the business because without you, it can't operate.)

- Do you have an "I" mentality versus a "We" mentality? (I do not give my employees as much credit for their ideas as I should. I believe that it will not get done properly unless I do it myself.)

- Do you have trouble getting your work done because you take on more than you can handle? (I am unable to properly delegate daily duties. I take on whatever I see that needs help to get done.)

- Do you have difficulty imposing self-accountability? (I let things slide because I get busy putting out day-to-day "fires," and no one is going to impose accountability on me, the owner.)

- Do you have knowledge deficiencies in areas where specialized knowledge is needed for you to do your job? (I don't understand how to manage sales people.)

Later in this book, I will show you how to develop Company Plans that will result in eliminating or minimizing work activities that involve your Personal Business Weaknesses and have the potential for "Big Picture" negative impact on your company. These Company Plans that articulate your Personal Business Weaknesses do not have to involve all your employees. Rather, you may decide to keep these plans only for your purposes, or possibly to a limited number of your employees.

## COMPANY WEAKNESSES OTHER THAN PERSONAL BUSINESS WEAKNESSES OF OWNER

One of the most common Company Weaknesses expressed by new TAB members involves management infrastructure. Mark Conroy expressed the following in his Company Weaknesses Statement:

- Lack of management structure and clarity of roles.

Even the most successful businesses have Company Weaknesses. You now have to look at the company's weaknesses in addition to your Personal Business Weaknesses that can have Big Picture impact. The following are starter questions to help you explore your Company Weaknesses. When you answer the questions, avoid using long narratives to explain or justify any Weaknesses. The key is to pinpoint the problems. In the following chapters you will learn how to develop the Company Plans that either remedy or neutralize Company Weaknesses.

### MANAGEMENT AND OTHER PERSONNEL

- Does your management have a culture of non-accountability? Ignoring repeated violations is an endorsement of an undesirable culture, and keeping employees who violate accountability and fight positive change, will destroy a culture.

- Are there any areas where management lacks skill that hinders company success? (E.g., communication skills, lack of diversity on the team, ineffective decision making, lack of innovation.)

- What shortcomings exist among your personnel in terms of skills or competencies? Consider factors such as technological skill deficiency, inability to follow directions, lack of initiative, or uncooperative attitude.

- Do you have employees who resist change? These employees generally don't come out and say they don't support something. They just don't do it. When you have resistant employees, you need to move them out of your company or get a commitment that their behavior will change.

- Do your company departments work well together in a spirit of alignment? Picture being in a rowboat with others and one person is rowing in the wrong direction, or at a different speed, or with different timing. The impact is inefficient movement forward, and exemplifies a common though significant Weakness in many companies—lack of alignment. Many companies don't succeed with their plans because they think that their employees are rowing their oars in the same direction, but they're not. This can be a serious Weakness.

## FINANCIAL FACTORS

- What financial factors weaken your company? (E.g., poor cash flow, inability to increase line of credit)

- How do your costs compare to your competition?

## SALES AND MARKETING

- What aspects of your marketing are least effective?

- What aspects of your sales process are least effective?

## MANUFACTURING, OPERATIONS AND DISTRIBUTION

- What operational issues keep you from reaching the success you want?

## PRODUCTS/SERVICES

- Are any of your products and/or services vulnerable to product/service substitution or commoditization?

- What, or who, is responsible for product or service failure?

- What advantages does the competition have over you?

- Looking towards the future, what else has the potential to become a critical Weakness?

As you review the assessment of your Company Weaknesses, select no more than five Weaknesses which have the greatest negative Big Picture Potential impacting your company's ability to reach your Company Vision Statement. These factors are the ones you will list in your Company Weaknesses Statement.

Let's take a look at Mark Conroy's written Company Weaknesses Statement, as it related to weaknesses other than the personal business weaknesses of owner:

- **Poor customer service** – Mark's internal feedback surveys from management and non-management employees identified that his employees evaluated the company's customer service level in a less favorable light than he saw it. His salespeople were then asked to talk to their customers face-to-face about Conroy Technologies' customer service. Based upon the survey feedback, along with the empirical information from the face-to-face conversations between his salespeople and his customer, he recognized that, although he had thought that his company delivered great customer service, he saw the truth of the customer service in a different light. The light shined brightly on the word "weakness."

- **Sales department** – Conroy Technologies' identified the following as Weaknesses in their Sales department: the top domestic person had been diverted to international sales; the company has poor sales training and sales training materials, and lacks a sales manager; the company lacks a sales methodology; the corporate website messaging is weak.

- Marketing department – Conroy Technologies has poor marketing materials; there is less brand awareness or mindshare than competitors; the company is too dependent upon an outside (and costly) marketing firm.

- Management weaknesses – The organization has poor project management, with poor execution of new product development; there is a lack of capable supervisory backups and an overall weak company culture.

## NOW START WRITING YOUR WEAKNESS STATEMENT

Once you have answered the applicable Company Weaknesses evaluation questions, consider the importance of each of your answers. Your Company Weaknesses have different degrees of potential negative impact for your company reaching the future you desire. Make sure your Company Weaknesses Statement is limited to those that are the biggest obstacles to attaining the Company Vision.

# COMPANY OPPORTUNITIES

## COMPANY OPPORTUNITIES RELATING TO THE BUSINESS OWNER

Opportunities that personally involve the owner (Personal Business Opportunities) often make up an important part of your Company Opportunities. That is why, when assessing your Company Opportunities, you should start with yourself as the owner. Many companies have reached greater success by creating Company Plans that take advantage of their owner's Personal Business Opportunities and turning them into a benefit for the company. The smaller your business, the more likely it will be that your Personal Business Opportunities will be of greater impact on your business.

A common Personal Business Opportunity is one that relates to family member employees or potential employees of the business owner. An example would be a family member potentially becoming an employee of the business.

The following are some questions you should consider in determining if you have Personal Business Opportunities that can have a major positive impact on your business:

- How can you improve your business leadership competency, such as joining a TAB peer advisory board?

- Are there family-related factors that create opportunities for your company? For example, is there a family member who has the ability to lead your business in the future and who might have an interest in entering your business?

- Would getting in better shape or losing significant weight increase the amount of energy you have to lead your company?

- Do you have any Personal Business Weaknesses that could be turned into Big Picture Potential opportunities if you neutralize them? Delegating the accounting tasks done by Andrew Arden to others in his small company freed up 20 percent of his work time to allocate for Big Picture Potential activity such as strategic planning.

- Are there any other Opportunities relating to you that can help your business be more successful?

Write down your Personal Business Opportunities that your business can take advantage of to improve your company. The most important of these Personal Business Opportunities should be listed on your Company Opportunities Statement. If you don't feel comfortable putting in certain Personal Business Opportunities for your employees to see, keep the points to yourself as your Personal Business Pocket Opportunities.

Bridget included the following excerpt in her Company Opportunity Statement:

- **I have potential investors who could provide funds for expansion.**

- **I have relationships with importers that could lead to a new distribution channel.**

As a business owner, you may see an opportunity to improve yourself in a way that can help the company, but you may not necessarily want to share it in the Company Opportunity Statement. For example, Bridget recognized that she would be able to contribute more to her company if she took certain technology courses because she did not have a strong background in technology. This was a Personal Pocket Opportunity for Bridget that she did not share in her written Company Opportunity Statement and she kept this in a locked personal file that only she could access.

## COMPANY OPPORTUNITIES OTHER THAN THE OWNER'S PERSONAL BUSINESS OPPORTUNITIES

Baker Manufacturing had contracts primarily with automobile companies such as General Motors, Ford, Chrysler and Toyota. In 2007, Bridget shared her concern about what was happening to the automobile industry. One of her fellow TAB Board members recommended that she consider hiring a former colleague, an out-placed executive who was experienced with manufacturing aircraft parts, including certification and sales. Bridget hired the out-placed executive as part of a course-changing plan that capitalized on the opportunity. The new executive opened up an entirely new market in the aircraft industry using many of the same skill sets and machinery that already existed in the company. This course-changing plan started with recognizing an opportunity.

## SOME OPPORTUNITIES HAVE TOO MUCH RISK

Mark Conroy saw an opportunity when he was offered a contract with a national company that would result in more than 50 percent of his revenue coming from that new customer. His brother Doug didn't think he should take the opportunity because of what could happen if he was dropped as a supplier, and he thought the company would be too dependent on one customer. Mark ignored his brother's warning and greatly expanded the size of his warehouse. He also acquired millions of dollars worth of sophisticated equipment to service the contract. He said it was finally his chance at "big money."

Not long after the building expansion was complete and the new equipment was installed, with very little notice, the company switched to another supplier. Mark was left with excess capacity and higher fixed costs, greatly hurting the company financially. The sad thing is that if Mark had listened to Doug, he would have heeded his advice to not expand without a long-term contract from the prospective new customer. Mark also ignored his own belief system of not having more than 20 percent of his company's sales volume with one customer.

## THE FINAL DECISION ON OPPORTUNITIES IS YOURS TO MAKE

I saw an opportunity for my real estate development company, Sun Development Company, to build Bernadette Square Shopping Center in Columbia, Missouri. I would be able to finance the development with a low-interest industrial revenue bond. I called a meeting to discuss the opportunity with my Sun Development Company management team. They explained their reasons why it would be a bad idea for us to take on the project. One of my executives mentioned the difficulties of the configurations of the site and problems relating to the land development, such as storm drainage and rock. He also said that no one in Columbia had received an industrial revenue bond, low-interest financing for a regional center, and that if tax-free bonds were available, one of the local developers would have already gotten them. Bottom line, he felt we were wasting our time even attempting to get the bonds.

The points made by the management team were very valid and showed what had to be overcome. But, they were not sufficient reasons to forego the opportunity. We applied for and received the tax-free financing that had never been given before in that area for our type of project. The project went on to become very successful.

## QUESTIONS TO HELP YOU IDENTIFY
## NON-PERSONAL BUSINESS OPPORTUNITIES

The following questions are designed to help you identify non-personal Company Opportunities which have potential to move the company closer to the vision of success. Your answers will help you identify Opportunities that have the potential for the greatest positive impact on your business.

## MANAGEMENT AND OTHER PERSONNEL

- What opportunities could you take advantage of to strengthen the skills of your management team and other personnel? (E.g., online training classes, seminars and mentoring?)

- Is there potential to upgrade personnel in your company? During the Great Recession that started at the end of 2007, there were many formerly successful and highly qualified business executives that found themselves out of work. Like Bridget, many TAB members have taken advantage of this opportunity to "upgrade the gene pool" of their personnel.

## FINANCIAL FACTORS

- What current financial opportunities exist that could potentially benefit your company, such as refinancing real estate at a lower interest rate?

- Should capital expenditures be re-allocated for uses that bring about greater financial positive impact?

- What are the worst case/best case budget scenarios for the opportunity ROI?

- Is there an opportunity to reduce your company's

taxes? At one time, Tipton, as well as every other retail chain in Missouri, was required to pay a tax on the inventory they had on a specific date every year. None of the other states where Tipton operated had a similar tax. I created an organization named the "Missouri Merchants and Manufacturers Association," which was comprised of other members of the business community who I had organized into a cohesive voice for eliminating the inventory tax. This effort ultimately resulted in a Missouri state constitutional amendment that ended the inventory tax.

## SALES AND MARKETING

- What industry trends exist that your marketing and sales efforts can leverage?

- What consumer buying trends could have a positive impact on your company sales?

- Is there the potential to sell additional products/ services or new products/services to current customers/ clients, or should the company look to new customers?

- Can your sales process be improved to help your sales team communicate your offer?

- What strategic alliance/partner opportunities exist? (E.g., acquaintances may be interested in coming into the business or becoming a strategic partner.)

- Is there a new technology or distribution channel to market your goods or services? (E.g., social media opened up a whole new world of marketing opportunities for many businesses.)

- What are you customers' future needs?

## MANUFACTURING, OPERATIONS AND DISTRIBUTION

- What operational improvement opportunities exist for your company?

- Are there opportunities to reduce expenses or production time?

- What new technology is available, or will soon be available, that may be able to lower company costs or speed production? (E.g., new software for client management.)

- Is there a need to improve or change your distribution methods?

- How do your manufacturing capabilities compare with your competitors'?

- What processes, if any, does your company currently provide to your customers, clients or users that may be provided more effectively by outsourcing?

- Can you improve your procurement or procedures,

qualification rules and information systems for vendor management?

## PRODUCTS/SERVICES

- Are your major competitors vulnerable in relationship to any specific products/services on which you can capitalize?

- What technology or market changes create a new product or service need? (E.g., a smart phone application)

- Are there markets that could be entered easily using the company's current areas of excellence and capabilities?

Bridget put the following in her written Company Opportunities Statement in addition to the Personal Points listed earlier:

- Increase brand awareness via social networks like LinkedIn and Facebook, and exhibit at targeted industry vertical Expos.

- Increase marketing and sales efforts for "back-end services" by delivering ancillary repair services.

- Test employing in-house telemarketers to set appointments with new customer prospects.

- Improve initial and continuing sales training of sales staff and upgrade sales personnel.

## BIG PICTURE POTENTIAL

Determine which of the Company Opportunities, whether owner-related or non-owner related, have the greatest Big Picture Potential to take your company to the future Company Vision you desire. These are the opportunities that need to be in your formal written Company Opportunities Statement.

# COMPANY THREATS

## COMPANY THREATS RELATING TO THE BUSINESS OWNER

Andrew Arden suffered two heart attacks within a few months of each other. Consequently, during his "Look in the Mirror" for his company, he identified his heart problem as a Personal Business Threat that could significantly affect his company in a negative way. Because he faced the Threat and made plans to neutralize potential impact from the Threat, his company not only succeeded, but prospered.

Bridget Baker listed the most important Threat to her business her concern that if anything happened to her, no other management employee is ready and able to run the business. Her daughters did not want to be in the business and her grandchildren are too young to join the business. The smaller your business, the greater the potential impact your Personal Business Threat can have on your company. Many small businesses are extremely dependent on their owners, though even the largest of privately owned businesses are impacted by the business owner.

There may be times that you will identify a Threat to the business that you do not want to share with management. You may decide to keep this in your "pocket" rather than including it in your Company Threats Statement. For example, one of Mark Conroy's sons who worked in his business had previously dealt with a drug problem. His son's drug problem had caused major issues, not only among family members, but also with other employees. At the time the Company Threats Statement was written, his son had finished rehab and was "clean." But, in Mark's mind, there remained the threat of a relapse. Mark decided that if the drug problem recurred, his son would have to leave the company. This was a Threat to the company because there was no one else trained to do his job. Although Mark identified the Threat of relapse, he kept it in his "pocket" and did not share it with the leadership of the company.

The following are some of the questions you should consider in determining if you have Personal Business Threats that should be identified in your Company Threats Statement:

- Are there potential problems within your marriage or domestic partnership that could have a negative impact on your business success? (E.g., spouse is business partner and marriage is failing.)

- Are there potential problems with your family member employees (children or other relatives employed in the business) that could negatively impact your business's success? (E.g., substance abuse of child in the business.)

- Are there potential elder care issues with parents or in-laws that could negatively impact your business success? (E.g., Taking care of an elderly parent will take time away from business, or financial cost of providing for them reduces capital availability for business.)

- Is there someone trained to take over your business if you become incapacitated or die? Do you have key person insurance that will protect the company and pay for the hiring of someone to run the company until it is sold?

- What financial risks leave your business exposed? (These are non-related business loan payments that could result in the bank going against personal guarantees affecting cash availability for business.)

- What additional personal Threats exist that could have potential negative impact on your business?

Be sure to put these threats in writing. If you don't feel comfortable putting some of these Personal Business Threats in writing for your employees to see, keep the information for yourself as your "Pocket Threats" element.

Bridget Baker included the following as her Personal Business Threats, but she kept these in a file that she did not share with her management team:

- 30 pounds overweight, which could cause health problems

- Marriage unsteady

- Husband believes I should be stay-at-home mom

- Husband's job may one day involve his relocation

## COMPANY THREATS OTHER THAN PERSONAL BUSINESS THREATS OF OWNER

I want to share with you some examples relating to Company Threats that will help you better understand how important it is to identify the Company Threats in addition to Personal Business Threats of the Owner. Arden Construction faced the Threat of competition from a large custom home builder. Andrew realized that if his smaller businesses expected to succeed against this giant, he would have to offer better service and create a system by which the company could react faster than the competition to new construction trends. He looked for ways to sell his services in as differentiated and more personable way as possible. As a result, he had his employees trained to provide a great level of customer service, unusual in the construction industry.

Many companies have a sales process that does not include web sales and are faced with Threats from web-based competition. They cannot eliminate the new competition. Instead, they need only ask, "How am I going to react to it?" Baker Manufacturing, for example, which had been successful for several decades selling its products via telemarketing, started to face new competition when the Internet created the ability for potential buyers to buy at lower pricing for similar products via the web. The Threat couldn't be eliminated, but early awareness of the Threat resulted in the company focusing its resources on creating its own web presence. It soon began offering its entire inventory via the web and was able to compete very effectively with the new competition.

Doug Conroy ran the software division of Conroy Technologies. His sales manager, Bill, who had been with the company for over a decade, was a major contributor, generating most of the company's large account sales. When Doug's biggest competitor lured Bill away, Doug found his business in a tough spot because he had no one qualified to fill Bill's shoes. Doug was forced to step in and devote himself to selling and managing the sales force while he searched for new help.

Not only did Doug abhor the task of selling, but this new task also the changed his day-to-day work focus and severely limited the time he had for focusing on activities with Big Picture Potential, as well as taking several months to find and train a new sales manager. If Doug had created a Company Threats Statement, he would have seen the importance of preparing for the Threat by creating a plan that would neutralize the impact if Bill left. A common Threat for many businesses is the potential of a key employee leaving when there is no one else in the company whose skill set fits the role just right. Doug also might have seen the importance of establishing a covenant preventing employees from competing in the event they leave the company—what is typically called a non-compete clause.

The following questions will help you identify potential Threats your business may be facing. Remember to look at it with clear eyes rather than answering according to wishful thinking.

**MANAGEMENT AND OTHER PERSONNEL**

- Will your company be hurt if a key manager quits?

- Is there a potential shortage of key non-management employees?

**FINANCIAL FACTORS**

- Will higher interest rates greatly impact your company?

- Does your company have principal cost increases that are tied to cost of living increases as defined by the US Index? (Such as a union contract with raises tied to cost of living increases.)

- Will a drop in dollar valuation raise your cost of raw materials?

- Could your company lose any of its trade credit or borrowing loans?

- Does your company have adequate corporate liability insurance?

**SALES AND MARKETING**

- Are there trends that may negatively affect the nature of the competition you face, such as commodity sellers like Wal-Mart or other big box stores?

- Is there a possibility of key suppliers beginning to compete directly?

- Are your sales too dependent on one customer?

- Manufacturing, Operations and Distribution

- Can international events result in a shortage of raw materials needed by your company?

- Is your business an "easy-entry" business for new competitors?

- Are there technological changes on the horizon that your company needs to accommodate or leverage?

- Products/Services

- Is the market for your primary product/service contracting?

- Are competitors able to under-price you?

- Are you unable to under price competitors or otherwise compete more effectively?

- Is your company exposed because you are not protecting your trade secrets and intellectual property?

When developing your written Company Threats Statement, identify three to five Threats, but no more than five, with the potential to have the greatest negative impact on your company's future. Keep in the statement only those potential Threats that can have significant impact on your company and that have the possibility of keeping your company from reaching the Company Vision. These are the factors you will use to create your Written Company Threats Statement.

Let's take a look at what Bridget identified as the non-owner related Threats in her written Company Threats Statement:

- **Competition alternatives available online at lower prices because they do not have a highly commissioned dealer network**

- **Possible new Government regulations for manufacturing**

- **Only nine years left on patents**

Ask yourself which of your identified Threats are the biggest obstacles preventing the Company from attaining your Company Vision Statement. Take the time to choose which of the Threats – whether they are owner-related or company-related – have the greatest potential to prevent your company from reaching the future you desire. These are the Threats that need to be in your formal written Company Threats Statement.

All the same principles and problems from non-alignment of co-owners relate to all the other company Statements. For example, co-owners need to be in alignment with Company SWOT Statements before sharing their mutually agreed upon company SWOT Statements with non-owner management. It is essential that they reach a mutually acceptable compromise before the drafts of the SWOT statement are shown to management; otherwise, "sides" or "factions" will develop with some management supporting one owner's views and other supporting the other owner.

## TAB BOARD REVIEW OF COMPANY SWOT STATEMENTS

Your fellow TAB Board members and Facilitator/Coach will give your Company SWOT Statements a "devil's advocate" review as well. For example, sometimes business Opportunities aren't always obvious. Opportunities may be in front of your face waiting to be grabbed, but we don't see certain Opportunities because we are so ingrained with how we see our own company and the industry in which we operate. Sometimes you need ideas from those outside your industry to bring them into better focus.

The flip side of this coin is that it is common for TAB Members to ask questions that result in the business owner seeing that they should pass on certain Opportunities. Bridget Baker told her TAB Board one morning that she was excited about opening a new plant to produce certain parts her company used, rather than contracting with a supplier. She pointed out that even though her company had no experience in producing these parts, nor could it control the supply and quality of the parts, the move would be an asset for her company; she believed her company could save significant money by manufacturing these parts. Luckily, her fellow TAB Board members convinced her that if she were to divert company financial and human resources away from present commitments relating to her Company Driving Critical Success Factor (DCSF).

Plan, the Company DCSF Plan was bound to fail. Moreover, they pointed out that her company presently did not have the sufficient expertise to handle the new production plant.

Bridget also shared her draft of Baker Manufacturing's Company Strengths Statement with her TAB Board. The statement reflected the marketing department as one the company's Strengths. During the TAB Board meeting, Bridget, who was deeply involved in company marketing activities, passionately explained why she thought that Baker Manufacturing Company's marketing efforts were so outstanding.

TAB Board members asked questions relating to marketing methods used by her company, as well as the results of the methods. The TAB Board members then expressed that they did not agree with her view of marketing being a Company Strength. Instead, the members explained that they saw it as a Company Weakness for Bridget's company. This was because the amount of dollars being spent by her company on marketing was far too much as a percentage of the annual revenue of her company, in the manufacturing field. They suggested that the company engage an outside marketing firm to bring needed areas of expertise to the company or, instead, the company should hire a full-time marketing executive. The suggestion to hire the marketing executive was followed and the advice of her TAB Board turned out to be effective.

## SWOT STATEMENT REVISIONS

Periodically, major changes in circumstances take place that are so significant in nature that they require changes to factors identified in your Company SWOT Statements. It is not uncommon for there to be major changed circumstances, such as a void created by an important manager who is no longer with the company, which would require changes to your Company Statements.

# ELEMENT 2:
# **CONCLUSION**

The road to success is rarely flat. Pedaling up the hills ahead, at times, seems daunting. But, if your company evaluation shows that the hills can realistically be climbed, you'll know you can reach the top. Once you get in the habit of evaluating your business by "Looking in the Company Mirror," the hills ahead will seem far less intimidating. You'll avoid taking a route that leads you to hills that are insurmountable for you to climb. Looking in the Company Mirror will make it easier for you to ride along the path towards your dreams of success. In fact, like most business owners who take the time to Look in the Company Mirror, you'll probably notice that the more you use the Blueprint company evaluation SWOT process in your company, the easier and more time efficient you become in developing the strategic plans you need to lead your company to success.

# ELEMENT 3: COMPANY PLANS
# INTRODUCTION

The third element of the Blueprint process is creating your company Strategic Plan. You, the business owner, are the key to making the Blueprint strategic planning process part of your company culture and keeping it consistently moving forward. Blueprint strategic planning will not work within your company unless it is embraced completely by you.

Business leaders can easily get caught up in the daily grind of their businesses, unaware that they are in a reactive mode, instead of standing back, assessing the situation and making decisions based upon strategic thinking. Yet, the reality is that business leaders who proactively develop strategic plans and lead the implementation of these plans are much more likely to achieve greater business success and greater enjoyment as a business owner.

Before you create a Company Plan you need to identify the foundation for each Company Plan. This involves the identification of those factors that are most critical to the success of your business. Each of your Company Blueprint Strategic Plans will focus on solving or satisfying one factor that is so critical to the success of your company that it can be viewed as a Critical Success Factor (CSF).

Once you have identified the CSF that will be the foundation for a Company Strategic Plan, you will develop four separate but inter-related statements for your Company Strategic Plan. The first statements for each of your Company Strategic Plans are written goals, which when successful, will satisfy one of your company's Critical Success Factors (CSF). In many ways you can look at goals as simply a CSF, which is conceptual in nature, rewritten into clearly written measurable language with timelines and responsible parties. The second Company Plan Statement consists of identifying Strategies that conceptually show how you will achieve the Goals. The third Company Plan Statement consists of written Action Plans for implementing each particular Strategy. The fourth Company Plan Statement consists of the Tactics that have to be completed by each employee responsible for completing a Tactic needed for the Action Plan to succeed.

# CRITICAL SUCCESS FACTORS:
## THE FOUNDATION FOR COMPANY PLANS

Every company is faced with factors that are critical to the success of the company. Identifying these Critical Success Factors needs to be done before creating written Company Strategic Plans. Business owners are too eager to move into action right away. They tend to do this before taking the time to identify what plans their companies should be focusing resources on, before their company plans are sufficiently developed.

In contrast, the Blueprint process requires that before you start the formal planning process, you must identify the factors most critical to successfully bringing your Company Vision to life. Your company's Critical Success Factors are the base upon which all Blueprint plans in your business should be built. Each of your written Critical Success Factors provides the solid platform upon which you build each Company Plan.

Just like a house, your Blueprint plans are only as strong as the foundation. You can construct and live in a house without a foundation; however, if your house is not secured to a solid foundation, chances are if a storm comes along you will lose your house or, at a minimum, the house will be severely damaged. A well-constructed plan, like a well-constructed house, will help your business successfully face the challenges that comes its way.

Therefore, the foundation of each of your Company Plans starts by you answering the question of what is "X" in, "If X does not take place, my long-term dreams for my business, as expressed in my Company Vision Statement, will not be achieved." Another way of expressing this is to ask, "What are the most impactful factors that could keep my Company Vision Statement from happening?"

Your Company CSFs will be unique to your company because they are so directly related to your unique Company Vision Statement. Keep your answer to the "X" question simple and conceptual. For example, one TAB member, upon reviewing his written Weaknesses Statement, identified "X" as follows: "If I don't proactively address the weakness in company upper management, my Company Vision will not be achieved."

Your company's CSFs are conceptual and non-measurable; satisfying those factors is essential to your company's success. Identifying CSFs show you, the business owner, and your employees, where all of you should best direct your individual and collective time and energy.

Each potential CSF needs to be challenged by asking yourself whether your company has the capability to achieve the CSF. For example, you may identify a CSF to sell a new product, which may have the potential generate great profits, but it may be unachievable because it requires human or financial capabilities that are beyond your company's current capacity. A review of your Company SWOT Statements, discussed in Element 2, can help you determine if the CSFs for your company are realistically achievable. Business owners often change a Company Vision Statement after looking at CSFs and determining his/her dreams for the company as being unrealistic.

## KEY CSF POINTS:

- Profit alone cannot be a CSF because profit is as much a part of a for-profit business as the act of breathing is to your survival.

- CSFs are conceptual in nature and do not entail measurements, time lines or dollar amounts.

## TWO TYPES OF COMPANY CSFs

There are two types of Company CSFs to consider when developing your written Company CSF Statement. The first involves the owner's business-related involvement in the company. The smaller the company, the more likely the most important factors critical to the success of the business will be highly dependent on the efforts of the owner. The other type of Company CSFs is not dependent on the owner. They includes company non-owner related factors involving such things as the need for improved marketing, the development of a new unique product, sales, improved distribution efficiency, or any other factor critical to the success of your company that is not related specifically to you as the business owner or your family.

## COMPANY CRITICAL SUCCESS FACTORS RELATED TO BUSINESS OWNER

Andrew Arden identified the most critical factor for the success of his business as being the need to spend more time on things that could have "Big Picture" impact upon the success of his company. Andrew Arden explained that one of his most beneficial company plans was to get to a point where 75 percent of his work time was to be focused on activities that used his Strengths and all his other work-related activities at 25 percent or less. His company made great strides forward, and he got more satisfaction from his involvement in the business when the plan was achieved. Andrew said, "I was amazed at how many of the day-to-day tasks I thought only I could take care of that were successfully delegated to my employees."

I could not help but notice how big the smile he directed at his wife became when he finished his story by saying, "Within a year of implementing my Plan, I had the time I needed to focus on growing the business – which is more successful than ever – and get my relationship with my wife solidly back on track." The Company Plan worked so well that it ultimately resulted in reducing his time at work to a four-day workweek because his "Big Picture" projects generated increased company growth and profit. These results would not have happened without a Company Plan that was focused on using his time at work to bring about greater positive impact on his company.

At this time, ask yourself whether there a critical factor related to you, the business owner, or a member of your family who is an employee that needs to be addressed before your long-term vision for your company's future can become a reality? If there is such as factor, as there was for Andrew, write it down in your Company Critical Success Factors Statement.

## COMPANY CRITICAL SUCCESS FACTORS NOT RELATED TO BUSINESS OWNER

Your next step is to identify CSFs that are not related personally to you. Bridget Baker identified a CSF for her company, which did not personally involve her. This CSF was the need to significantly bring down manufacturing costs per unit in order for her products to be priced more competitively. She recognized that the company's current equipment was under-utilized, and felt that the company could triple its production without having to invest in any additional equipment or building space.

The following questions will help you to identify your company's critical success factors. While not all encompassing, these questions will help you to uncover some of the most common Critical Success Factors for your business.

- What new product, service or process requiring development is needed? (E.g., to compete more effectively, we need a low-priced entry-level product with fewer features.)

- What area of excellence or customer/client impact needs to be prioritized by your company? (Customer loyalty.)

- What market area needs expansion? (We need to sell regionally rather than just locally.)

- What better use of capacity or efficiency is needed to reduce per unit cost? (We need to excel at increasing output from costly machinery.)

- What improved technology or know-how is needed? (Newer high tech equipment to get greater plant cost efficiency.)

- What improvements in your sales and marketing methods, practices or personnel are needed? (Improve our electronic marketing efforts.)

- What improvements in your distribution method or ordering system effectiveness are needed? (Website must provide more efficient electronic ordering by our customers.)

- Are changes needed in the location of your headquarters or distribution plants? (To be more competitive, we need to expand the size of our distribution plant.)

## CREATING YOUR WRITTEN COMPANY CSF STATEMENT

The time has come to put together your business owner-related and non-business owner-related CSFs for your business and create your written Company Critical Success Factors Statement. No matter what stage of growth your company is in, try to identify up to five CSFs in writing.

## PICK THE RIGHT CSF OR CSFs TO BE THE FOCUS OF YOUR COMPANY PLANS

After you have completed your Company CSF Statement, pick the CSF or CSFs that should be the focus of your Company Plans. Critical Success Factors identified that are not addressed by companywide plans may become the foundation for plans that will be worked on by individual managers, teams or departments of your company, rather than Company Plans that are focused on by the entire company. If a proposed company plan is 80 percent or more the responsibility of only one department, it should not be a companywide plan. It should be a department plan.

## DRIVING CRITICAL SUCCESS FACTOR (DCSF)

You will be ready to start writing your first Company Strategic Plan when you identify which of your CSFs is the most essential factor to your company's success. In some cases, it is the CSF needed for your company to successfully excel and, in other cases, it may be what is needed to survive. That factor becomes your company's Driving Critical Success Factor, which we refer to as the DCSF. Your DCSF holds the greatest economic benefit for your company, and will be the Factor around which your first and most important Blueprint Company Plan will be built.

A Driving Critical Success Factor for Baker Manufacturing was: "To make greater use of expensive manufacturing equipment that is owned, but underutilized so that manufacturing can be done without increasing fixed equipment costs and, in turn, create greater profits."

Another example of a Company DCSF was my first Driving

Critical Success Factor, which was the foundation for my first TAB Company Strategic Plan: "TAB needs to attract qualified, experienced business professionals to become TAB-certified Facilitator/Coaches who have the ability to be trained to provide peer board and coaching services, using my system." It's easy to see why I picked the above DCSF when I started TAB, since it was essential to my Vision of building TAB into the world's largest franchise system providing peer advisory and coaching for business owners.

Your DCSF, like the Baker Manufacturing and the TAB Boards examples above, must have the potential to have a major positive impact on your company. A DCSF must not have the potential only for low positive economic impact. Too many small and mid-size businesses mistakenly misallocate company resources by pursuing CSFs that, if achieved, will have too little impact on their company.

Periodically, when certain specific impactful events take place, you will also need to rethink and redefine the Driving Critical Success Factors, and in turn, the Company Goals and Plans on which your company is focusing.

# COMPANY PLAN OVERVIEW

## COMPANY STRATEGIC PLANS WILL HAVE A POWERFUL IMPACT ON YOUR BUSINESS

If you are like most business owners, you don't do a great job of developing written strategic type Company Plans. In fact, according to the results of a TAB survey, over 60 percent of new TAB Member businesses did not have any written Company Plans in place when they joined TAB. For most of those who did have written plans, the plans were more action-oriented than strategic in nature.

Bridget Baker shared with me that she didn't realize how off track she was from achieving her Personal and Company Visions until she started her company going through the process of developing Company Strategic Plans. She explained to me, "I was so tied up in my day-to-day matters that I was not doing the things needed to direct me towards my dreams. I was working like a dog and was constantly exhausted." Then, with a downward glance, she added, "And my husband, who was fed up with the fact that I was always working, was ready to divorce me."

I asked her when she started to see a difference, to which she replied, "Within months of when I put my first Company Plan into writing, with company goals, strategies and action plans. Before I had a lot of good ideas, but I wasn't running my business strategically. My Strategic Plans created a positive energy with strategic direction for my managers and me."

## THE FOUR STEPS OF THE WRITTEN BLUEPRINT COMPANY PLAN

Now that you have completed your Critical Success Factors Statement, and determined the DCSF to be the foundation of your first Company Strategic Plan, it is time to start creating the plan. There are four steps to a written Company Strategic Plan, and these four steps rest on the foundation of a Critical Success Factor, as shown in the following Blueprint Company Plan Pyramid:

TACTICS

ACTION PLANS

STRATEGIES

GOALS

CRITICAL SUCCESS FACTOR

The four steps consist of:

- Identifying Goals, realistically attainable within 36 months, that will, when achieved, satisfy the Critical Success Factor;

- Identifying up to five Strategies per Goal that conceptually show how you will achieve each Company Plan Goal;

- Identifying up to five Action Plans for each Strategy that show how you will implement the Strategies; and

- Identifying an unlimited number of Tactics for each Action Plan that details the Tactics that will make each Action Plan successful.

If you have Company Plans in addition to the DCSF Plan, each of these other Company Plans will be written with the same steps used to create your DCSF Company Plan. This means you will need to identify the CSF, Goals, Strategies and Action Plans.

## LIMIT THE NUMBER OF COMPANY PLANS TO WHAT YOUR SIZE COMPANY CAN HANDLE

One of the most common mistakes made by business owners is creating too many Company Plans for their company's infrastructure's to handle. The larger your company, the better it can manage achieving more than one CSF, and therefore, more than one Company Plan. For Large companies, you may have the infrastructure and other resources to create and carry out companywide plans to address up to five CSFs. However, you should finalize your DCSF Company Plan before writing your other Company Plans.

A Mid-size company should limit the number of CSFs to pursue with Company Plans to no more than a couple of CSFs, because of limited infrastructure to work on to many plans. The smaller your company, the more likely it is to that the company will only be able to effectively have company-wide focus on only one Company Plan, the DCSF Company Plan.

Most Small-size companies are better served by focusing on one Company Plan to achieve one CSF at a time, because they do not have the available resources to address several Company Critical Success Factors at one time. A Small-size company should limit itself to focusing on satisfying one CSF at a time. This is important because Small-size companies will probably not accomplish the goals of any their Company Plans if their resources are spread too thin by working on more than one plan at a time.

When Andrew Arden created a complex plan for his business with five Strategies for the Company Plan and five Action Plans for each Strategy, it totally overwhelmed him and de-motivated him to a point where very little was accomplished relating to the Company Plan. The due dates on the Action Plans were constantly missed. The more often this happened, the more discouraged he became.

Andrew's TAB Board members recognized that there were too many things that needed to be done by Andrew himself with his company Action Plans and felt that there was no way he was going to get them all done. Andrew's Board members explained this to him. They suggested that he focus on and commit to the board only one Action Plan that could reasonably be done during the following month.

Things turned around when he was convinced to have only a few Strategies, each having one Action Plan that could be fulfilled within 30 days. Going to this bite-sized approach enabled Andrew to commit to his TAB Board and Facilitator/Coach on what would be accomplished before his next monthly TAB Board meeting. The board convinced him to focus on just the two most important Strategies and only two Action Plans for each Strategy, for a total of four Action Plans.

Prior to this bite-sized approach, Andrew was embarrassed at his monthly TAB Board meeting when he had to share what had not been done. This bite-sized approach allowed him to 'save face' with his peers. During the board meeting after his first bite-sized 30-day commitment, he was motivated to make the Company Plan succeed. Having this additional accountability to his board gave him extra motivation to make sure he could come to each meeting being able to share that he had accomplished his Action Plan that he had committed to at the previous meeting.

The reality is that if small company owners, such as Andrew Arden, are able to accomplish their 30-day Action Plan objectives, they will stay motivated and will see noticeable improvement in their businesses within months of starting a Plan. Even if they fall short of hitting their Company Plan Goal within its designated time frame, they will see measurable monthly progress. Seeing this value for their company keeps them disciplined and committed to using the Blueprint process.

If your company focuses on too many Company Plans at one time, bandwidth limitations may result in not enough company resources being allocated to your Driving Critical Success Factor

Plan. If this problem of insufficient allocation of needed resources is standing in the way of your Company's DCSF Plan being met, you should delay putting into effect lesser, even though important, Company Plans.

During the first few bi-weekly group meetings Bridget Baker had with her management team, which consisted of her sales manager, operations manager and controller, she was unhappy when she reviewed the progress of her Company DCSF Plan. When the plan was developed, the managers agreed on the timeline for every tactic needed to achieve the Goal of the Company DCSF Plan. The problem was that none of the projected results were taking place. She asked her managers why the Plan was not succeeding. The controller expressed his opinion that the company's budget was not large enough to sufficiently fund some of the Action Plans needed to achieve the Goal of the particular Plan. Bridget had made the mistake many business owners make of spreading company resources, human and/or financial, across too many different Company Plans, instead of first allocating whatever was needed to make the DCSF Plan succeed. Results picked up almost immediately when she changed course and decided that there would be company-wide focus on only one company-wide Plan, the Company DCSF Plan, until she saw great progress with the plan.

Even though Mid-size private companies have more managers to make a Plan succeed, rather than heavy dependence on the business owner, most of these companies are better off focusing on only one Company Plan, the Company DCSF Plan. Because of the reduced dependence on the business owner for implementing the Plan, Mid-size companies are more likely to be successful with multiple

Strategies – up to five – for each DCSF Goal, and up to five Action Plans for each Strategy. Taken to its maximum amount, this involves 125 different Action Plans. This is no small number. Consequently, even Mid-size companies (with the additional personnel resourced to implement Plans) rarely are able to tackle successfully the maximum number of Strategies and Action Plans possible.

# GOALS

## THE GOAL

*"The most important thing about goals is having one."*

*—Geoffrey F. Abert*

The first step in creating a Company Plan is to identify a Goal or Goals that will satisfy the Critical Success Factor that you have already identified as the foundation of the Company Plan. As the Company Plan Goals must be realistically achievable, you'll need to consider things such as your company's human resources, equipment capacity, and your company's financial ability to achieve the Goals.

Each Goal must be measurable and achievable within a three year period. The measurements must be of a type that can be easily tracked by Key Performance Indicators (KPIs) that can be reviewed on a regularly scheduled basis. For example, Conroy Technologies compares their monthly new client acquisition to last year's performance from the same month.

Your Company DCSF Plan should bring about a company-wide focus on achieving this most important Company Goals. Your DCSF Goals need to have company-wide commitment and focus. Your written Company DCSF Plan Goals should become a well-memorized mantra known by all your management and employees. The Goals identified to satisfy the current Driving Critical Success Factor of your company should generate the greatest company-wide focus because it is the pinnacle of achievement for your most important company plan. Every employee should keep the DCSF Plan at the forefront of their day-to-day thinking, so they don't ever lose track of it.

For example, Andrew's company developed a Company Plan Goal relating to "increase customer satisfaction." The goal was to "get a minimum of 80 percent satisfied to extremely satisfied rating from our current customer base within three years." Bridget's company developed a Company DCSF Plan Goal that involved increasing company sales threefold within three years, through the use of independent sales representatives, while cutting manufacturing cost per unit. Every employee in their companies had to know these written goals.

Your Company DCSF Plan must allocate the necessary company resources to accomplish the goals and satisfy your DCSF. Resources for your DCSF Plan should be the last area to cut out. Therefore, you must firmly decide on the resources needed to successfully satisfy your DCSF Goals and to give your DCSF Goals preferential treatment with those company resources, before you create Company Plans to achieve any of your other CSFs. To do this, you need to complete your written DCSF Company Plan for achieving the Goals, including all the Strategies and Action Plans and Tactics that need to be set in motion to get results identified in your Goals. This written plan needs to be completed before creating/writing any other Company Plans.

## A GOAL FOR EACH COMPANY PLAN

Don't pick the Goals for your Plan like a poker player who bluffs. In poker, players may hold on to risky cards in hopes of a long shot, even though there is a good chance of losing. If you want to see results, plan for the most likely hand to be a winner. Overestimating your company's capability by trying to focus on unrealistic Goals can make you a loser.

Focus on Goals that can be realistically achieved in a maximum of three years, although they may be reached much earlier. The Blueprint goal-setting process for privately owned businesses is quite different from the strategic process traditionally employed by large publically owned businesses, which have the infrastructure to plan several years or more into the future. This type of long-term goal setting typically does NOT work for privately owned businesses because the nature of business owners requires more immediate results to maintain their focus. I have seen too many cases in privately owned businesses where goals longer than three years were never achieved because the business owner got sidetracked. Business owners are less likely to get sidetracked by Goals that take no more than three years to achieve.

Also, the Goals must clearly define the benchmarks that need to be attained while moving toward the full goals being completed, again all within three years. The Goal's benchmark measurable phases, may be something such as a 10 percent increase in sales the first year, a 20 percent increase the second year and, a 30 percent increase by the end of the third year. It is easy to see how these measurements give checkpoints for you to see if the results are on course.

The Goals must be measurable and written in a way that gives your employees a basis on which to judge achievement. This also helps focus their energies. Take the time to write the Goals, for each of your company Plans, as clearly as possible.

## IDENTIFY THE GOALS MOST CRITICAL TO ACHIEVING YOUR CSF

The following questions will help you identify the Goals most critical to achieving the CSF you identify as the foundation for your Company Plan. These questions are meant to assist you in identifying your Goals, but are not all-inclusive and will not apply equally or at all to every business owner.

### IF YOUR CSF INVOLVES CUSTOMER SATISFACTION:

- What measurable target for customer satisfaction do you need?

- What measurable quality attributes for your product/ service is needed?

### IF YOUR CSF INVOLVES OPERATIONS:

- How much do your operating costs need to adjust for

your primary product/service?

### IF YOUR CSF INVOLVES FINANCIAL FACTORS:

- What improvement is needed in cash flow?

- What debt-to-equity ratio is needed?

- What is needed for current asset and liability ratios?

### IF YOUR CSF INVOLVES SALES:

- What annual revenue ranking do you need to have in your industry to satisfy your CSF?

- What does your company need in measurable improved rates of repeat sales or retention of customers/clients?

- What increase in sales is needed for each of your major product or service classifications?

- What is a reasonable rate of sales increase for the next three years?

## WRITTEN COMPANY GOALS STATEMENT

As you begin to write the Goals for your Company Plan that best describes what needs to take place to achieve your Company CSF, make sure to add measurements, timelines and accountability to your designated CSF.

# STRATEGIES

## COMPANY STRATEGIES

Strategies are the conceptual guidance system that brings you to the realization of your Goals. They are the compass on your Blueprint Bike that lets you know you are "on course." For every Company Plan Goal, you will need to develop strategies, with the number of strategies being dependent upon the size of your company. For example, large companies may be able to effectively handle as many as five strategies for each Company Goal.

The company evaluation information disclosed in "Looking in Your Company Mirror," as explained in Element 2, often called the SWOT picture, will help in creating the strategies to achieve the Company Goals that you have just identified. Your Company SWOT will point out what best utilizes your company strengths, neutralizes weaknesses, takes advantage of opportunities, and prepares you as best as possible for addressing threats outside your control.

A review of your Company SWOT Statements can also help

you determine key aspects of what is needed in the strategies for your Company Plans. One strategy for a Company Goal may involve making greater use of the areas in which your company has Strengths. Is there a strength you identified in your Company Strengths Statement that, if used to a much greater degree, could be helpful to your company's success in reaching a goal?

Take note of your company Weaknesses, especially those that exist to a greater degree in your business, than they do for your strongest competitors. Ask yourself whether you need strategies to neutralize these Weaknesses for your Company Goals to succeed. As my father used to say, "The last thing you want to do is to get in a fight in a business area that is a weakness for your company, but a strength of your competitor."

Is there an opportunity that you identified in your Company Opportunities Statement that will help you make a Company Plan Goal a success? Remember that Bridget's DCSF involved the problem of the company's current equipment being underutilized. Bridget saw the opportunity to engage sales representatives to increase company sales. Bridget's company plan had a strategy involving the engagement of independent sales representatives with the goal of tripling the company's production within three years, without having to invest in any additional equipment or building space. The increased sales that resulted from Bridget's plan brought down the manufacturing cost per unit by 15 percent in year three.

Is there a threat that you identified in your Company Threats Statement, which if not addressed or prepared for by your company, can derail your company's chances of reaching the success of a Company Goal? Think of Kodak's position in the world as a developer of film and the impact of digital cameras, which do not need developing. Kodak filed Chapter 11 bankruptcy. However, the good news is that they ultimately closed down their developing plants and made significant course changes that resulted in them becoming a leader in affordable digital cameras. Somewhere along the line, they shifted their business in a way that took advantage of the opportunity presented by technology for affordable digital camera photography.

## STRATEGIES REQUIRE CREATIVE THINKING

Approach the development of Strategies with the maximum amount of creativity. Be prepared for resistance from others who might respond to new strategy ideas by invoking the popular adage, "If it ain't broke, don't fix it." This kind of thinking has stopped many business owners from developing Strategies that move a company from good to great.

Creating Strategies is, in many ways, an art. This kind creativity is based on past experience and specialized knowledge of your company, your industry and your leading competitors. All of these can provide a secure sense of guidance in creating Strategies, but instinct and intuition also play an important role in developing "out of the box" Strategies. This type of creative thinking can only occur when you remain open to breaking the status quo, and comes from those who are not locked into the common thinking of your industry.

Remember that your Strategies are to be conceptual, not detailed or specific. In other words, when writing your Strategies Statement, save the details for your Action Plans, this will be both specific and measurable, and show the point person who is responsible for driving its success. Your Action Plans must show one and only one person as the point person who is responsible for driving its success.

Watch out for Strategies that require capabilities outside of your company resources. This is especially true when it comes to Strategies that are focused on taking advantage of your Opportunities. Take the time to look realistically at how easily you can bring a capability to your organization. If it's not readily doable, don't make it a Strategy. Finally, when you have created your strategies in support of a Goal, stop and ask yourself, "If my company achieves these Strategies, will the Goal be accomplished?"

### STRATEGIES QUESTIONS

The answers you provide to the following questions will help you identify the best Strategies for the Goal that is the focus of your Company Plan. Note that these questions are meant to assist you in thinking through how you approach your Strategies. These questions will not apply equally to every business owner, but are meant to be thought provoking for the type of questions you should be asking yourself while you develop your strategies.

### MARKETING:

- What is unique or distinct about your business that can be leveraged to create a strategy to attain your Goal?

- What are the marketing strategies used by the leading

competitor in your industry from which you can learn or adapt to your company?

- If you are operating in more than one geographic market, what are the common characteristics of the geographic markets in which you are operating successfully that can be used as a Strategy for further expansion?

- What Strategy for developing your company's marketing and operational infrastructure is needed to successfully smooth the progress of desired growth?

- What are your market segmentation and niche strategies?

- What aspects of your pricing strategy should change?

- Are there market opportunities that offer strong upside potential without an unreasonable risk?

- What strategic alliances should your company develop?

**SALES:**

- What strategies for sales compensation programs need to be changed?

- What strategy for sales management could increase results?

- What strategies for sales training may make your sales

staff more effective?

- Are there strategies that will increase customer retention?

- What strategy might yield increased revenue from current customers?

- What strategy might be used to increase referrals from your satisfied customers?

- What additional capabilities or tools does your sales force need?

## PRODUCT IMPROVEMENT:

- What strategy should be used to address any unsuccessful products/services?

- Is there a strategy for adding products or service features that you can offer to your existing customers or clients?

- Is there a strategy for adding features to your products that would create greater value for your products compared to your competition?

- Is there a strategy for improvements that create greater value than your competition offers?

## ORGANIZATIONAL:

- What strategies will make the organizational structure

of your business more effective?

- Is there a strategy for improving the corporate culture involving improvements, such as cutting down on company bureaucracy and minimizing company politics?

- Is there a strategy that will improve fluidity of communication between departments and from bottom to top?

- Is there a strategy for improving your management infrastructure?

- Is there a strategy for improving your technology?

- Is there a strategy for improving employee relations?

- What is your strategy for eliminating poor performers among your employees?

- Is there a strategy for employee development that would facilitate business growth or improvement?

## WRITTEN COMPANY STRATEGIES STATEMENTS

Now it's time to create your Company Plan Strategies Statement. Each of the Strategies must be conceptual, rather than measurable, and follow a clear and easy to understand way to reach your Company Plan Goal.

# ACTION PLANS

Action Plans identify what needs to be done to satisfy a specific stated Strategy. There should be no more than five Action Plans for each of your Strategies.

Action Plans break down what may seem to be an overwhelming task into small, manageable units, using the Blueprint SMART criteria. An Action Plan SMART criterion requires that the Action Plan be Specific, Measurable and Achievable, have parties that are Responsible for results and include a Time frame. Let's take a look at the SMART criteria:

- SPECIFIC: Spell out exactly what needs to be done, by whom, and when it will be done, step by important step. Specific Action Plans also address resource issues such as funding, staffing, and equipment needs.

- MEASURABLE: Knowing up front how results from your Action Plans will be measured is the only way you will know whether or not you are on target. There are different methods for measuring the results. These measurements must be clear and objective, such as sales increasing by a certain percentage.

- ACHIEVABLE: Your Action Plan must have a realistic chance of success, otherwise, the Action Plan will be demoralizing to the party responsible for its success.

- RESPONSIBLE PARTY: One specific person, not two or more people, must be designated as the Responsible Party who has committed to implement a specific Action Plan. The Responsible Party must have the authority, as well as the responsibility, to see it through to success. It's not enough to state that you or someone else will do what it takes to see an Action Plan through. Action Plan accountability may be designated yours, or any of your employees. The Responsible Party for the Action Plan will manage the Action Plan process.

- TIME FRAME: Establish a realistic Time Frame for how and when an Action Plan is expected to be completed. For example, is the Action Plan expected to take six months to be accomplished? If it isn't accomplished on time, the lack of success should trigger responses for making it happen. Always include the outside date for each benchmark of your Action Plan to be completed. Benchmarks with closely tracked deadlines are the monitors that will tell you if things are going as planned or not. The person responsible for the completion of an Action Plans needs to provide self-accountable estimates of the amount of time it will take to complete the Action Plan.

## ACTION PLAN QUESTIONS

The following are examples of questions that Blueprint Coaches have asked when helping a business owner create a company Action Plan. The business owner's Strategy was to, "to add salespeople," and which was developed to achieve a Goal of increasing company sales by 20 percent during year one of operations:

- How many new salespeople will need to be hired this year to achieve the sales increase Goal of 20 percent during year one?

- Is the money budgeted to train the salespeople and compensate them before they generate sales?

- What tools (such as behavioral surveys and credit checks) should be used during the interviewing process for new sales employees in order to identify those likely to become better performing salespeople?

- Who will manage the salespeople and how often will sales results be reviewed?

- How will the sales growth of your business be financed?

The size of your written Action Plans, excluding tactics, like other formal written Blueprint Statements, should be no more than 100 words.

## LIMITED NUMBER OF ACTION PLANS FOR EACH STRATEGY

Even with a Large-size company, there is a limit of five Action Plans for each Strategy. I've worked with business owners who insisted that five Action Plans were simply not enough to accomplish a particular Strategy. It turned out that it was much more effective to keep the limit of five Action Plans and instead review the Strategy because it is likely to be too complex. Try, instead, to break the Strategy into two or more separate Strategies.

The smaller your business, the more the amount of Action Plans should be limited for a particular Strategy. A Small-size business may only be able to effectively handle a couple of Action Plans.

*Note: Plans that are manageable are the Plans that can happen.*

## ACTION PLAN QUESTIONS

Answering the following questions will help you develop your written Company Action Plans Statements. Not all of these questions will apply to any particular Action Plan Statement you may be developing.

## OPERATIONS

- What is needed to differentiate your company's primary

products or services from those of your industry competition?

- How can you lower the risk of product failure, thus lowering the buyer's expected cost of failure, as well as your cost of returned products?

- How can you improve your product by improving any of the following: appearance, installation cost and/or ease, price, ease of use, versatility, user and/or maintenance cost, durability, speed, size, material quality, accuracy?

- How can you lower your prices based on improved internal efficiency?

- How can costs such as delivery, installation or financing be lowered?

- How can you process orders faster?

- How can you lower labor costs?

**AFTER YOU HAVE COMPLETED A DRAFT OF EACH ACTION PLAN, CHECK TO SEE WHETHER:**

- Goals are specific enough?

- Expectations are realistically achievable?

- Evaluation dates for verifying that the Plan is on schedule and on track have been identified?

- Clear measurement methods are employed?

- Expected results are communicated to specific people or teams?

- New equipment and personnel will be needed?

- Someone is assigned to manage the action plans on a company-wide basis?

- If Action Plans succeed, will the Company Strategy be accomplished?

**KEY POINT:** Have all needed human and financial resources been realistically identified that are needed for the Action Plan to succeed? Only after doing this can you forecast and budget your foreseeable financial requirements. The reality is that the smaller the company, the more often this budgeting and forecasting is not formally done. If your company doesn't have the wherewithal to do formal budgeting and forecasting properly, at least develop a "ballpark" budget and forecast number before finalizing each of your Company Action Plans.

## IT IS YOUR TURN TO CREATE YOUR COMPANY ACTION PLAN STATEMENTS

Now it's your turn to create a Company Action Plan Statements for each of your Company Strategies. Begin by listing Actions that will satisfy the Strategy on which you are focusing. Then narrow down your list to only those Actions that are realistically likely to satisfy the Strategy.

## CHAPTER 18

# TACTICS

Within each Action Plan, there probably will be many Tactics that need to be implemented by you and individual employees for the Action Plan to succeed. There is no limit to the number of tactics, other than the practical constraints of your company's infrastructure, to be able to complete tactics in a timely manner. Tactics are the commitments that you and your employees will follow to bring about a successful Action Plan. Tactics are both specific and measurable; they pinpoint the actions required by specific responsible parties, within set parameters, so that you can measure the results or impact of the Tactics.

Tactics have relatively short deadlines within which they must take place. An example of such a Tactic is for the Director of Marketing to solve the problem of an employee on his team who is hurting the company because of a passive-aggressive style. The Director of Marketing is responsible for implementing the Tactic, which is just one task of the Action Plan.

For smaller companies, it is important that some of the tactical commitments have short (no longer than 30-day) completion deadlines, so that the employees can see that some Tactics are being completed.

Don't confuse the Action Plan Statements with the many Tactic assignments to specific employees that must be achieved for the Action Plan to succeed. Tactics can be assigned to anyone in the company, although authority for updating tactical due dates is limited to an employee, generally a manager, who is responsible for the specific Action Plan.

The party responsible for the Action Plan must assign and clearly communicate Tactic responsibilities under the Action Plan, as well as expectations to the parties responsible for the Tactics. It is important to always document the person responsible for completing each particular Tactic of the Action Plan.

A Tactic that calls for a manager to hire an assistant, for example, must include the deadline for doing so. This must be done in order to verify the Tactic dates are being met.

There is no word size limitation when capturing in writing your Tactics to carry out an Action Plan. There is no limit to the number of words to define the Tactics needed to carry out each of your Action Plan Statements.

The following example is a list of questions to develop when writing a Tactic, in this case for hiring sales staff:

**TACTIC QUESTIONS**

- Who will create (or update) a job description for the salespeople, and by what date must it be completed?

- How will the salespeople be recruited?

- How will the salespeople be compensated?

- Who will conduct the interviewing?

- What selection criteria will be used?

- By what date must the salespeople be hired and start employment?

- By what date must the salespeople start and complete training?

- On what skills or product information will the new salespeople need to be trained and who will do the training?

- Who will create the training programs and when is the deadline?

- What minimum sales results are expected from each salesperson and within what time frame?

**WRITTEN ACTION PLAN STATEMENT WITH TACTICS FOR CONROY TECHNOLOGIES**

Let's look at one of Conroy Technologies' Action Plans that was based on satisfying a CSF that involved making its training program for users of its software one of the most effective in its field. This CSF had a Goal of attaining a minimum average of 80 percent good to outstanding rating from those taking the training. This satisfaction level needed to be achieved within three years. The following shows written Strategies and excerpts of Action Plans and Tactics developed by Conroy that led to accomplishing the Goal.

| Goals | Strategies | Action Plans and Tactics | Responsible Person(s) | Target Date |
|---|---|---|---|---|
| Have a training program for new users of our software that gets a minimum of 80% good to outstanding rating from facilitator/ coaches in the training. December 3, 20__ | 1. Expand the number of onsite training days and create online training programs to allow more time for interactive training. | 1. Develop PowerPoint and other materials for all training sessions.<br><br>2. Practice training support sessions before using with a training class.<br><br>3. Create short videos and other visuals to be embedded in PowerPoint.<br><br>4. Move selected PowerPoint presentations into online training modules with exams | 1. D.<br><br>2. D<br><br>3. D<br><br>4. S | 1. April 29<br><br>2. May 7<br><br>3. Sept 6<br><br>4. |
|  | 2. Create Survey to be completed by trainees after each session to measure training effectiveness and satisfaction of trainees | 1. Create survey questions | 1. C. | 1. May 7 |
|  | 3. Create pre-training materials that need to be studied by trainees in advance of initial training, along with online open book test | 1. Slides, handouts and case study materials to be created to train new facilitator/coaches on how to use with members. | 1. C. | 1. Before May Training |

## TOOLS FOR CREATING AND TRACKING COMPANY PLANS

TAB members have access to a TAB Web-based application, which allows the easiest, most efficient way to create their Company Plans, including the tracking of the results of the Action Plans and to make changes to the Action Plans. However, if you are not a TAB member and don't have access to our TAB Web-based Business Builder's Blueprint application, it is easy to create the statements via Excel spreadsheets or even Word documents with points that are kept simple, clear and concise.

# INFORMAL ADVICE ON COMPANY BLUEPRINT STATEMENTS

Developing your Company Strategic Plan Statements requires a high level of commitment and self-discipline on your part, as the business owner. But no matter how committed and self-disciplined you are, you may still be able to adjust and improve your Company Strategic Plan Statements for certain people whose opinion you respect, who I refer to as informal advisors, to get their feedback. You have a world of information concerning your business in your head, but sometimes seeing things from a different perspective will challenge your thinking in a way that significantly improves your Company Strategic Plan Statements.

Your informal advisors must all understand that your privately owned business exists to satisfy the long-term desires of you, the owner. If they don't understand this, their advice will be much less valuable to you.

Consider who you might value as an informal advisor to help you further develop your company strategic plans. With many privately owned businesses, this informal advice will come from either certain selected employees, usually high level managers within your organization, and/or from fellow TAB Board members, as well as your TAB-Certified Facilitator Coach.

## EMPLOYEES AS INFORMAL ADVISORS

Even if your company is a Small-size company, such as Arden Construction, you may have an employee or employees in whom you have confidence to use as informal advisors for their comments on your Company Strategic Plan Statements. At Arden Construction, Andrew used his controller, who also had operations responsibility, as an informal advisor to challenge his Company Strategic Plan Statements. With Mid-size and Large-size companies, you will probably have one or more trusted high level executives in your company whom you can ask for feedback on your Company Strategic Plan Statements. Large-size companies should have top level executives who can serve as an established, top level management team to help formalize all the written company Blueprint Statements, as well as to make your company plans succeed. If you own a Large-size company, Element 4 of this book will show you how to form and make the best use of a management team.

Your informal advisors often bring to the table varying perspectives that come from having a different set of eyes and ideas on your Company Plans than only yours. Although you want feedback from your informal advisors, the final decision on your Company Plans is not handled in a democratic way. The reality is that if you, the business owner, are not satisfied with any aspect of any Company Plan, you won't support it fully. You have to believe in your own Company Plans!

Informal advisor employees will often see things in a different light than you. It's up to you to ensure that these informal advisor employees show respect to each other and appreciate each other's areas of expertise. An environment should be created by you so that any of your informal advisors who are also employees will not be hesitant to share their views about your Company Strategic Plan Statements, particularly the Company Plans, even if they disagree with you or their fellow informal advisors.

When Bridget Baker first started using Blueprint, she shared with her top two managers the drafts of her first Baker Company Blueprint Plans, asking for their feedback. At first she was very charming and personable, although hard-driving. Ten minutes into the meeting, one of her managers challenged the achievability of her proposed Company Goal. Bridget switched from a charming business owner to one who blew up and defended the particular Action Plan with yelling and cursing. Then, just as suddenly, she returned to her charming persona.

How do you think that Bridget's outburst affected the atmosphere for the rest of the informal advisors? What are the chances that she received total openness from her employees after that? Not too good, I'm afraid. It should not be surprising that the employees did not challenge or offer feedback on anything else in the meeting.

During our first coaching session after the meeting with the two managers acting as informal advisors, Bridget told me, only half jokingly, that she was totally behind the idea of employee meetings, but with this caveat, "As long as they understand that in my company, the only ideas of the employees that count are those of the owner, the owner and the owner."

I explained to Bridget that her managers could not serve as informal advisors on her Company Blueprint Plans unless she created an atmosphere where her employees could be open with her. Bridget agreed to listen openly to challenges to her perspective of what should be identified as the Driving Critical Success Factor for the company. After hearing her employees informal challenges to her view about what should be the company's DCSF, she would then think through the justification of her position. At the next monthly coaching session, Bridget commented to me that, "I'm glad I allowed my managers to challenge my thinking because it resulted in a change in what we all see now as our Driving Critical Success Factor."

Within most companies, the owner has one or more employees that the owner can share things with in a more confidential way, getting feedback from these informal advisors. Of course, you do not have to take the advice of your advisors. It is, after all, your company.

## FEEDBACK FROM TAB MEMBERS AND TAB-CERTIFIED FACILITATOR COACH

Regardless of the size of your company, if you are a TAB member, you will be able to get informal advisory input from your TAB Board and your TAB-Certified Facilitator Coach. Part of the role of each TAB member is challenging your Company Strategic Plan Statements. Fellow TAB members will commonly challenge your Goal, for example, by saying something like, "That Goal may be exactly what you would like to attain, but do you have the people to do it?" Many TAB Members have left TAB meetings changing their mind about a particular Goal or ready to adjust expectations of the Goal because they realized during the TAB Board Meeting that the Goal wasn't realistically attainable.

## PERSONAL POCKET FACTORS THAT AFFECT YOUR COMPANY'S STRATEGIC PLANS

You may have a Pocket Factor, such as the desire to bring your son into your business, that, for whatever reason, you do not want expressed in the company's formal strategic plans. Your informal advisors may be able to help with the integration of your son into the business if they know this information. They may make the transition easier on him and for your non-family member employees.

Share the Pocket Company Plans with your informal advisors to the greatest extent you feel comfortable. Realize that the more you share, the more your informal advisors can help you achieve your dreams as expressed in your Personal Vision Statement. If you don't share your Pocket Factors, expect that your informal advisors might disagree with some of your ideas and conclusions because they do not possess all the information.

## TYPES OF CHALLENGES BY INFORMAL ADVISORS TO COMPANY CSF AND STRATEGIC PLAN STATEMENTS

Your informal advisors should challenge you about such things as the following:

- **Is the Driving Critical Success Factor you have identified the right DCSF?**

- Are the Goals to achieve your company DCSF realistic?

- Can your company accomplish the Strategies for the Goals with the resources your company has, or has budgeted to have?

## MULTIPLE OWNERS

Co-ownership offers more challenges to developing aligned Company Strategic Plans, particularly when the ownership is equal. It is essential that there is agreement among co-owners to reach alignment on their Blueprint Plans, in order to keep their company from harm due to conflict among co-owners that directly or indirectly affect the business. If there are co-owners and one is a majority owner, the majority owner's views will override the opinions of the minority owners if they can't agree on a compromise for the Company Strategic Plans. But, once the plans are put to bed, there must be full support among the owners without sharing with non-owner employees the dissent that they shared with their fellow owners.

ELEMENT 3:
# CONCLUSION

You, the business owner, are the one who must ingrain the importance of Blueprint strategic business planning into your company's culture. Blueprint strategic business planning must be totally embraced by you and your management team to get maximum benefit. Once Blueprint strategic thinking is part of your company management belief structure, "Blueprint planning thinking" will trickle down through your entire organization, and knee-jerk reactions and seat-of-the-pants decisions will stop happening. Blueprint strategic business planning will impact every single component of your business, including how you make important business decisions and how every aspect of every job is accomplished. Using the Blueprint strategic business planning process creates timely strategic change and decisions that will power your company's journey to greater success.

Blueprint strategic planning must be totally embraced by you and your management team to get maximum benefit. Your executives must both understand and follow the protocols required in the Blueprint strategic business planning process for Blueprint to work most effectively to achieve your personal dreams and dreams for your company.

# ELEMENT 4: MAKING IT HAPPEN

# INTRODUCTION

Element 4 focuses on using all of the tools available to strategically lead your business, while embracing and balancing the hands-on nature required of a business owner. A business owner who is a Strategic Business Leader, is always leading his or her business towards making his or her vision for the long-term success of the company a reality. This long-term vision of company success is referred to as a Company Vision. When it is identified in writing, it is a Company Vision Statement. Using Business Builder's Blueprint is the key to achieving the Company Vision that has been identified by the business owner. Achieving the success is referred to in Blueprint as literally "Making It Happen." Using the techniques of Blueprint will provide the formula you need to reach your vision of success for your company.

You, as the business owner, are the key to leading your company to your vision of success for your company. "Making It Happen" requires more than good ideas; this element requires disciplined follow-through and timely adjustments to the plans so that your company is reacting to situations faster, with more flexibility and more aggressiveness than your competitors who may not be using Blueprint.

Having great company Strategic Plans is not enough to make your business reach your dreams of success. You have to use the Blueprint leadership techniques, processes, and methods to make these plans succeed. In Element 4, I will show you how to use Blueprint to address the challenge business owners have in finding a balance between strategically leading their businesses and the hands-on involvement that is often necessary. I will also show you how and when to make the all important course changes in the plans your company is making.

Business Builder's Blueprint is not a "one size fits all" way of running a business, but rather, one in which it is essential that you stay true to who you are. By this I mean staying true to your basic personality or behavior nature, while using Blueprint leadership techniques, processes, and methods.

Also, Blueprint leadership techniques, processes and methods need to be customized to best fit the management makeup and size of your company. Regardless as to the size of your company, Blueprint will not be embraced by your management unless it is first embraced by you. In this element, I will show you how to adapt the techniques, processes and methods to your size company, which have been identified in this book as Small-size, Mid-size and Large-size Companies.

In Small-size companies, the business owner typically has to be much more hands-on than with Large-size companies because of the absence of any significant high-level management presence. The owner is the one who reviews the results of employees responsible for Company Action Plans. In Mid-size and Large-size companies, it is more likely that the companies will have several managers, maybe even a group of high level managers, who collectively act as the management team (Management Team), who will be primarily responsible for reviewing the progress of your Blueprint plans and modifying them as needed to succeed. Reviewing the progress requires identifying the tools and Key Performance Indicators (KPIs) to be tracked by your company to manage information so that timely modifications take place.

In Element 3, I explained how to identify the critical success factors (CSFs) that are critical to the success of your company. I also explained the importance of moving to the next step, which is to identify the CSF that is so essential to the eventual achievement of your Company Vision that the Company Vision will not take place if that particular CSF is not achieved. This CSF, which is most important to your company's success, is referred to in Blueprint as the company's Driving Critical Success Factor (DCSF). The first and most important of your company plans (Company Plan(s)) will be achieving your Company DCSF, and this plan will include a Plan Goal(s), Plan Strategies and Action Plans.

Most business owners use Blueprint to lead their company into action, following the Strategies in their Company Plans, as soon as the Action Plans are developed. They set things in motion with a high degree of confidence that successful results from these Strategies will attain the Goal(s) of each Plan. But projected results don't always happen the way you would want. That's just a fact of life for any business, whether small or large.

Blueprint is to be used to lead your company to meet obstacles head on. Focus on company results with course changes and modifications, in a timely manner, as needed to ensure your company success. Being a Business Builder's Blueprint Leader means you will react quickly to challenges and opportunities. A Business Builder's Blueprint Leader's quick reaction approach gives you and your company a competitive advantage. Sometimes strategies need to be modified, eliminated or replaced. Sometimes the changes that need to take place are deep within the tactics of the Company Action Plans. The only way to be on top of this hands-on level involvement is with Company Action Plans and the results of the Tactics for the plans that are monitored on a regular basis. Typically, either you or other management in your company will have to review and adjust your Action Plans, as needed, or you won't achieve the results you want.

# 20

# YOUR STRATEGIC FOCUS

As the Strategic Business Leader of your business, you are the key to ensuring that all the strategic factors involved in your business are the best strategic factors for your company at that particular time. When you recognize that they are not the best strategies, you need to make sure your company changes course to put more effective strategies into place. It is your responsibility to identify the important strategic changes your company needs and then lead the way to your company embracing these strategic changes. One strategic change alone can have a major impact upon your company's success.

Changing Course generally takes place only after you rethink your SWOT statements, CSFs, and the Goal(s) and Strategies of your Company Plans. Things change, and changed circumstances often mean a new or different direction for your company. Sometimes the changed factors are so significant that it may even result in changing your company's course from focusing on your current company DCSF plan to a much different plan.

## MANAGEMENT ALIGNMENT ON STRATEGIC DIRECTIONS

As the Strategic Business Leader, it is your responsibility to make sure that all of your managers are aligned in support of your Company Plans, particularly your Company DCSF Plan. Let's look at how Bridget Baker brought about much needed alignment on her company's strategic direction. Bridget decided on a Company Plan that changed the way her company dealt with prices. For decades Baker Manufacturing sold its products at prices that could be negotiated, but recently she thought it might be a good idea to stick to prices that were non-negotiable. Bridget discussed her ideas about a new pricing model with all her managers and encouraged them to express their views on the Company DCSF Plan. Her sales manager expressed his fear that company sales would be hurt. Bridget explained that eliminating negotiated pricing would benefit the company because customers would feel more confident that they were getting the right price the first time. She added that it would require a period of adjustment for those used to negotiating, but the change would ultimately result in increased sales and profits.

She found out a week after the meeting that her sales manager was telling other employees that he thought the new Plan would "destroy" the company. Bridget quickly met with this sales manager and explained to him that his comments of concern were not acceptable after the decision to move ahead with the Company Plan. She also explained that if he could not support the Company Plan for revising the pricing model, he should not be part of the organization.

As it turned out, the strategy Bridget developed for changing the company pricing model was a great success. Being proactive in getting your executives to support your Company Plans, once it is put in place, is often the difference in their success or failure. Alignment of all your management in their support of your company's strategies is essential.

## ANNUAL CHANGING COURSE REVIEW

In the next chapter, I will show you examples of how changed circumstances that occur at any time may cause you to rethink the strategic way you are leading your business. But whether or not these types of changes take place at any time during the year, it is important to conduct annual reviews of your Company SWOT Statements, Critical Success Factor Statements and Company Plan Statements, excluding Action Plans and Tactics, which you are reviewing on a regular basis. Take the emotion out of the evaluation when you are considering whether or not to change any of these written company statements.

Annual reviews of these written Company Statements will help to pull you back from your day-to-day efforts putting out fires. These reviews will help you to take the time to focus on the implications of major changes in circumstances for which you may be aware, but haven't given enough thought to their potential impact. When conducting the annual reviews, take the time to get away by yourself to think about the course changes your company may need.

The annual review of key written company statements is much different than the weekly, biweekly or monthly review and revisions that you do throughout the year, relating to your Company Action

Plans. You will not be reviewing your Company Action Plans during your annual Changing Course review.

If your company lacks management level employees, your annual Changing Course review may involve just you, by yourself, getting away from your business to an environment where you have no distractions. This annual Changing Course review will start with looking at whether anything has occurred during the last year that is significant enough to consider a change to Company Plans.

## USING EXECUTIVES TO HELP WITH ANNUAL CHANGING COURSE

I take my bikes into the shop every spring to get annual tune-ups. The bike techs look at the various parts and analyze them to make sure they are lubed, not banged up and all are working well individually, as well as together. Having these technicians involved brings about a better tune-up than if I did the annual tune-ups by myself. For the same reason, your Changing Course annual reviews will be more effective if you have top-level managers help you with them.

The bottom line is that Small-size companies typically don't have top-level executives to help with your annual Changing Course tune-ups. As companies grow in size, there should be more executive level employees in your company with whom you feel enough confidence in, to consider them as informal advisors. If you have such executives, your annual Blueprint Changing Course review should involve retreats that include these executives as your informal advisors. During these annual Changing Course retreats, your executives should challenge your Company SWOT Statements,

CSF Statements and Company Plans – particularly the Goals and Strategies. Significant course changes commonly take place to your CSFs and Company Plans, as a result of changes made to your SWOT Statements.

Even with Mid-size and Large-size companies, a strain is placed on the company if all the executives are out of the company at the same time for several days. Consequently, annual Changing Course retreats with your executives will likely be a series of half-day or full-day meetings, with regular working days in between, so your executives are able to continue managing the business. This kind of scheduling minimizes the all-too-common excuse by executives that they can't spend the time away from work for strategic thinking because it will take too much time away from their day-to-day tasks. Annual Changing Course retreats should be held in a location where there are very few distractions.

Bridget schedules her annual retreat meetings with her managers for a half-day on a Saturday for the first meeting, and with the follow-up meetings during evenings, in order to minimize disruption of company day-to-day activities. By having the meetings at a retreat, it minimizes her managers being distracted by interruptions at work. During your Changing Course annual retreat time, your executives should be able to step back from the activities on which they are working, week in and week out, and instead focus on strategic matters.

## AGENDA OF ANNUAL CHANGING COURSE REVIEW

Before each annual Changing Course retreat, spend time on pre-meeting preparation. Write down your thoughts on potential changes to the statements that each of you think should be looked at, based on each of your beliefs. At least one week before the annual Changing Course retreat meetings, e-mail your executives who will attend the retreat to provide your thoughts on possible changes to your written Blueprint Statement mentioned above. This should give your executives enough time to prepare for the annual Changing Course retreat meeting with questions, challenges and suggested changes to your ideas.

At the beginning of your annual Changing Course retreat meetings, explain, in no longer than five minutes, what you see as the advisory roles and responsibilities of the executives/managers with whom you are meeting, as well as what you hope to achieve from the Changing Course retreat meeting. Your next step is to briefly go over the agenda for the meeting. Then share your views about each of the changes you are considering for your written Company Statements. Next, it is important to get their feedback.

Review your CSFs and reconsider which one is the DCSF for the company. Bridget Baker creates new SWOT Statements "from scratch" each year at her annual Baker Manufacturing retreats without reviewing her current year's written Company SWOT Statements. She believes it brings greater creativity than if she started with the current SWOT Statement and made some changes to them.

**WARNING:**

When you share written Company SWOT Statements drafts with your executives, do not list any Weakness that reflects poorly on a member of the executive team.

## CHAPTER 21

# INTERIM STRATEGIC COURSE CHANGES

Changing Course doesn't have to wait, and in some situations should not wait, until your annual review. There will be times when things change and you will need to react strategically and not wait for an annual review to change course in your company. Sometimes it is for a good reason, such as a Company Plan achieving its Goal(s), or an Opportunity development that wasn't previously available when you made your Company Plans, and which now offers the possibility to take advantage of the opportunity.

Other times, strategic Course Changes are needed because of reasons that are not particularly good, such as a company plan has failed. An all-too-common situation that causes rethinking of a company direction takes place when there is new or changed competition. Sometimes strategic direction needs to change because of something as basic as the loss or potential loss of a key executive, or the potential loss of a lease for the building in which your company operates. Unfortunately, when financial problems occur, they may require a time sensitive response. There are also situations in which you need to switch gears because of natural disasters or the loss of the company's major client.

## COMPANY PLAN HAS ACHIEVED ITS GOAL(S)

When an existing Company Plan has successfully attained its goal(s), it's time to eliminate that Company Plan. If your company DCSF plan has been achieved, a strategic decision needs to be made as to what your new DCSF plan should be. It may be designating one of your current Company Plans as the new company DCSF Plan. If a plan other than a company DCSF plan has been achieved, you may or may not want to add a new Company Plan Statement to replace the achieved Company Plan, or you may determine there is already a new Critical Success Factor your company needs to address.

## OPPORTUNITY DEVELOPS THAT WAS NOT PREVIOUSLY AVAILABLE

There will be times when your company has a new Opportunity that was not present at the time of your last annual Changing Course retreat. For example, an unexpected Opportunity to buy a small competing contracting company in Arden Construction's area became available. The Opportunity became available because the owner of the small contracting company decided to retire and sell his business. Andrew Arden decided to jump on the opportunity. He created a new Company DCSF Plan of buying the assets and clients of the former competitor. Andrew's previous DCSF Plan was moved down in priority because he felt that strategically it was no longer as important to the future of the company as taking advantage of the

Opportunity to buy the small competitor.

TAB's expansion plans for the United Kingdom originally involved having several master franchisees, each with a territory of approximately 20 million people. TAB changed this strategy because an Opportunity presented itself when an outstanding professional in the UK expressed an interest in helping TAB open up in the UK. The top executives of TAB met and made a strategic decision that we would have only one master franchisee in the UK if we were able to work out an agreement with this outstanding professional. Due in part to this change in strategy, TAB has had a very successful expansion into the United Kingdom.

## CURRENT COMPANY PLAN HAS FAILED

Often there is pressure from key employees to keep Company Plans in existence long after they should have been removed. They have become "Sacred Cows." Sacred Cows, in a business sense, involve plans and projects that no one is allowed to touch no matter how damaging their continued existence may be for the company. Employees may use such rationalizations as, "so much money has already been invested in the plan that we need to see it succeed." When in reality, eliminating such plans would only point out the failure of the executive who originally pushed for that plan. Sacred Cow Company Plans stay on too long because they are treated as sacrosanct, even after it is clear that the problems are very hard to fix, remove or change.

Bridget Baker agreed to a major company financial and human resources commitment to develop customized software to help Baker

Manufacturing operate more efficiently. The particular software had been pushed for by Mike, the Director of IT. Mike assured Bridget that the software would help company profits and the software would work well within one year.

The original budget for accomplishing the initiative was $50,000, plus a substantial amount of time by employees. Three years later, the company had spent several times the projected budget, and the software was still not useable by Baker Manufacturing. Mike kept telling Bridget that the product completion was "just around the corner," and gave all kinds of excuses, such as incompetent vendors who supposedly were to blame for the delays and budget overruns. Baker Manufacturing continued to put good money into a bad project while the budget ballooned. The problem was that Mike had his reputation and credibility on the line and was blinded by the reality that the software product was a huge failure.

After a monthly review with me, as Bridget's coach, Bridget said she did not want to let this project continue to suck more money from the company. She pointed out that after considering the payments to outside resources and the real cost of company personnel time spent on the project, over $300,000 was sunk into this software, which was still not working. So, Bridget eliminated that Company Plan, explaining to her employees, "It's time we cut our losses."

## NEW OR CHANGED COMPETITION

Competition does change, leaving in its wake those companies that don't adapt. Look at the evolution in the retail industry. Warehouse stores put small mom and pop retailers out of business.

Warehouses stores, in turn, were impacted by catalog stores. The catalog stores were then challenged by big box retailers. Sales on the Internet have impacted the big box retailers.

The time to start thinking about the needed strategic reaction to new or changed competition is the moment you become aware it exists. If your company faces a new significant Threat from new or changed competition, you won't want to wait until your annual Changing Course meeting to address this Threat. This is the time to call a special retreat to change your Company Plans.

Changed competition refers to any significant change taking place in your industry that comes from your competitors. Many companies have gone under because they kept on doing things the same way even as the new competition entered their market. Think of the impact of digital photography on companies like Kodak that provided non-digital photography products and services. However, also keep in mind my earlier reference to how Kodak, which some thought was edging toward obsolescence and had filed Chapter 11 Bankruptcy, changed the course of their basic business model to not only stay in business, but to become a leader in the affordable digital camera market.

Many companies avoid a course change when faced with new competition and instead, try to compete on cost alone. Unless you have deeper pockets than the new competition, this is a formula for disaster. The course change should take into account what your company can offer clients or customers that the new competition does not. In manufacturing, a staggering number of manufacturing businesses in the United States, Canada and Western Europe have changed course due to low-wage global competition. Low-wage global competition has also impacted non-manufacturing businesses such as technology companies.

Sales at Baker Manufacturing Company were greatly impacted when a major competitor switched from manufacturing in the USA to manufacturing with much lower wage costs in China. This switch to manufacturing in China allowed Baker's competitor to dramatically lower their prices on non-customized products on large manufacturing runs. As a result of the pricing pressure from Baker's competitor, there was a significant major impact on Baker's gross profits. Bridget made a strategic decision to focus her company's sales efforts on customers needing time-sensitive fabricated products that were not as price sensitive because the customers were more concerned with getting them fast, rather than at the cheapest price. The products manufactured in China by the competitor took much longer to get to the consumers.

There may be new products from your competition that make you reconsider whether you should be working on competing products. New software products from one of Conroy Technologies' competitors made completely irrelevant a plan that Conroy had worked on for a couple of years relating to developing a particular software product. Conroy was in the final stages of testing the new software product when a competitor launched a product that was faster and more robust than the product that Conroy was testing. In this case, Conroy's Company Plan was eliminated even though it had not achieved its goal.

## LOSS OR POTENTIAL LOSS OF KEY PERSONNEL

Conroy Technologies had operated successfully for decades without a strong local competitor. Eventually a competing company did enter their market and offered the same products and services. At the time, Conroy did not have non-compete agreements with their employees. Conroy Technologies experienced the loss of a key employee who had strong personal relationships with several key accounts that were responsible for a significant amount of Conroy's revenue.

After losing the key employee, a Changing Course style retreat was scheduled by the Conroy brothers with their informal advisors to address the concern of protecting the sales with key accounts. At the same time, they considered what should be done to prevent losing other key sales people. The Conroy brothers led their company executive team in developing a major Course Change that addressed, with a Company Plan, proactively keeping the above mentioned key accounts. The plan also addressed how to keep the company from being as vulnerable in the future to the loss of any key employee. This revised Company Plan included new financial incentives to salespeople, while simultaneously having them sign non–compete agreements prohibiting them from competing within 50 miles of Conroy's headquarters.

Are you too dependent on key personnel who have exclusive or almost exclusive relationships with your company's key accounts? Losing key employees cannot be controlled, but plans can be developed to both reduce the likelihood of losing them and to minimize the negative impact should the loss take place.

When a business is family-owned, the business is vulnerable to family relationship fallouts. This can include divorces of family members employed in the business, which can result in the loss of a key family member employee. In a similar manner, when the relationship between partners is ending, strategic plans need to be developed to address who will assume the responsibilities and authority of the partner leaving the business. When key family members or partners leave a business, a strategic plan is needed to address the effect on employees. If family members or partners have signed personal guarantees for loans or lines of credit, the business must also consider potential problems, such as how the departure of that family member or partner will affect the bank loans or lines of credit.

## LEASE TERMINATION

Andrew Arden was not concerned at all about renewing the lease on the building used by his construction company, even though he knew it was coming up in less than a year. However, several months before the company's lease renewal date, Andrew was informed by his landlord that the landlord would not renew their lease because the tenant next door wanted to expand. Andrew reacted quickly by deciding to replace the company's then current DCSF with a new DCSF Plan that had a Goal of leasing or buying a new building for his company.

## FINANCIAL PROBLEMS

A company may experience financial problems that did not exist during its last annual Changing Course review. The type of financial problem may range from potential loss of bank loans to a problem with cash flow. When financial problems crop up, a course change may be required to address the problem because financial issues have a tendency to escalate if not addressed in a timely manner.

At one monthly coaching session with her TAB-Certified Facilitator Coach, Bridget Baker pointed out her concern about a potential company cash flow problem. She had just received a cash flow projection that showed her company would experience cash flow problems within a few months if no action was taken. Bridget met with her team and led a strategic change in the company's philosophy towards collections. From that time forward, Baker Manufacturing has taken a much harder position on collecting and charging penalties for past due accounts.

## NATURAL DISASTERS

We have no control over natural disasters. The key to surviving these disasters is often dependent upon how quickly courses can be changed with Company Plans developed to face the changed circumstances. For example, Baker Fabrication's manufacturing plant was once located in a 100-year flood plain area. Unfortunately, during one historic flood, water entered their building and stood several feet high, making operations impossible. Certain equipment used by the business was not in working condition after the water subsided. Since the company was essentially shut down because of the natural disaster, Bridget had to immediately focus on a strategic decision on whether to move the equipment to a new location or to wait out the time necessary for her then current location to dry out and begin operating again. Her decision to purchase a new building and move the equipment took 90 days, which was amazingly fast. Yet, it is easy to see how this caused major strategic shifts in handling so many things from personnel matters, to communications with customers who were waiting for their products.

Another example involved a company that manufactured specific parts used by Conroy Technologies. The company, located in China, was devastated by an earthquake. Mark Conroy had to develop an emergency course change for finding another supplier of the parts or the hardware division would have been shut down. The strategic decision wasn't limited to just the interim needs because suppliers willing to gear up to supply the parts wanted a longer-term commitment.

## LOSS OF A MAJOR CUSTOMER OR CLIENT

Things change when a major client or customer is lost or may be lost. This situation may mean your company focus needs to change. If your company's sales are represented by a small number of accounts, loss of one of these accounts can have a dramatically large impact on your company. It is easy to say to business owners that they should have business models so that their companies are not dependant on one or a few accounts. It always is best to diversify your accounts so that you won't become vulnerable. Yet, the reality is, when a giant company like Wal-Mart, which could represent an enormous amount of revenue, knocks on your door and asks to be your client for most of your production, it is hard to say no.

Many companies have been destroyed because they were overly dependent on a major account and were not able to make a quick course change when the account dropped them or significantly reduced their order. In some cases, this happens because a key party with the account, such as a purchasing agent, changes jobs and the new purchasing agent gives the business to someone with whom there is an established relationship.

Arden Construction discovered that a local retail chain that accounted for over 50 percent of the company's annual revenue was going out of business. A new Company DCSF Plan, which involved a strategic focus to making the retail chain a smaller factor in Arden's annual revenue, became the priority of his company. Company-wide focus needed to shift from cost efficiency to new client acquisition.

# *22*

# "HANDS-ON" WHEN
# LEADING STRATEGICALLY

The reality is that most business owners will have some level of hands-on, very tactical involvement in leading their companies to success. You will probably need to do more than focus strategically on your Company Plans to make sure they succeed! In addition, you will probably do more than monitor the effectiveness of the strategies in the plans. Strategic Business Leaders unemotionally evaluate whether their Company Plans are working or need to be changed. This evaluation almost inevitably brings about a challenge of balancing this strategic level of leadership with more tactical or hands-on involvement. At times, every business owner is faced with the need to go deep with hands-on involvement.

This dilemma often involves the company DCSF Goal(s) because it is such an important focus of your time as the Strategic Business Leader. It is critical to keep your eyes on the Company DCSF Goal(s) and monitor the measurable Key Performance Indicators (KPIs) results versus projected results. In most cases, your company's

DCSF Plan Goal(s) has a limited number of key measurable results to track, sometimes only two to three items. If you achieve all of your KPIs, you will knock the Goal(s) of your Company DCSF Plan out of the park.

In Element 1, I talked about the Blueprint Bicycle, which has a front wheel of your Personal Vision Statement and a Rear Wheel of your Company Vision Statement. The degree of hands-on involvement as you drive your Blueprint Bicycle to its destination of your long-term personal and company success will be unique to you because of the following four factors:

- Allocation of company resources among Company Plans

- How well your company is succeeding

- The number of employees you have (including the number and quality of managers) to help you lead your business

- Who you are; your personal business-related Strengths, Weaknesses, Opportunities and Threats

**FACTOR 1: ALLOCATION OF COMPANY RESOURCES AMONG COMPANY PLANS**

One of the challenges that Strategic Business Leaders commonly face is the allocation of company resources between the DCSF Plan and the other Company Plans, department plans or team plans. While it is important you lead your company by keeping the priority on resources needed to make your company DCSF plan succeed, this doesn't mean that you drop all other needed activity within the company. Very often, you'll need to clarify for managers how much of their time and their department's time has to be diverted from the DCSF Plan to working on company, department or team plans, and the day-to-day needs of running a business.

For example, at Conroy Technologies, a company DCSF Plan involved a Goal of acquiring a certain amount of new clients. Doug Conroy was pleased with the progress of the DCSF Plan. However, at a certain point, he became dissatisfied with the quality control of the software development activities. He decided to create a department plan, in addition to the DCSF Plan, that he personally worked on to improve quality control. This plan required the involvement of certain departments, including marketing, which he tasked with developing certain surveys for his project. The marketing manager was torn between what he saw as the needs for the DCSF Plan and the diversion to working on Doug's quality control plan. Mark Conroy, who was in more of a CEO role, had to get involved, in a very hands-on capacity, to determine what portion of time the marketing manager could divert and should divert to Doug's plan. In making these kinds of hand-on decisions, you need to recognize that your company cannot do everything all at the same time, and determine what core areas must be the priority.

In some cases, these are individual tactics that are not part of a formal plan. Andrew Arden recognized at a certain point that his company needed a new marketing brochure aimed at a certain type of potential clients. The brochure wasn't part of his company wide plan. It was simply one of those tactics that often comes up and needs to be addressed. Since Andrew had no marketing department, he contracted with an outside marketing firm to create the brochure.

## CHAPTER TWENTY-TWO

## FACTOR 2: HOW WELL YOUR COMPANY IS SUCCEEDING

When things are going great in your business and plans seem to be succeeding, it's much more likely that you're going to be leading with minimal hands-on efforts. However, when a company's results are unsatisfactory, it is inevitable that business owners of every size business will revert back to their basic nature of trying to solve problems at every level. This happens often when the business owner feels things aren't being done as well or as fast as they could be done.

Regardless of the size of your business, you are likely to get involved at every level of your business. You will get involved anywhere you feel your efforts are needed to achieve success for the Company Plans. This is not the greatest way to develop your managers, but there are times when you simply have to do what is best for your company at that moment. There will be time later to mentor and to give your managers a wider berth.

It is not unusual for you to have a greater "hands on" involvement during a time of economic challenges, such as during the 'Great Recession' that started in 2007. During tough global economy periods, many TAB business owner members acknowledged at their TAB Board meetings that they needed to revert back to hands-on involvement to fix any problem, anywhere in their companies that they felt could be helped with their involvement.

## FACTOR 3: THE NUMBER OF EMPLOYEES YOU HAVE TO HELP YOU LEAD YOUR BUSINESS

The smaller the size of your company, the less likely it is that you will have managers who are able to help you lead your company. It is also more likely that you will be personally involved in monitoring your company results. In Small-size businesses, you may be alone in leading your company to the desired results. You will need to be the one with the ideas for making the changes needed to get company results in line with projections.

A Strategic Business Leader has to balance giving leadership vs. being hands-on with a Responsible Party for an Action Plan. In a Small-size company, it is very likely that you will be the one directly responsible for an Action Plan or will be meeting with the party responsible for a specific Action Plan (Responsible Party). If you own a Mid-size or Large-size company, it is more likely that your regularly scheduled Action Plan meetings will be led by the manager who is the Responsible Party for a particular Action Plan.

If you own a Large-size company, such as Conroy Technologies, it is less likely that you will be directly involved in managing Action Plans or Tactics. The larger your business, the more likely it is that you will have managers who can help you in your leadership role. Many Large-size companies have a Management Team, which provides major help in monitoring and revising Action Plan results as needed to achieve success. Leading your company to make your Strategic Plans succeed requires that you discipline yourself to stay focused on each Company Plan until the Plan Goal(s) is achieved.

## WHO YOU ARE: PERSONAL BUSINESS-RELATED STRENGTHS, WEAKNESSES, OPPORTUNITIES AND THREATS

As I mentioned earlier, the way you will drive your company's Blueprint Bicycle to its destination of your personal and company success will be unique in part because of who you are: your Personal

Business-Related Strengths, Weaknesses, Opportunities and Threats (SWOT). Changes to your leadership approach are likely to come about if you take the time to do an objective evaluation of your Personal Business Related SWOT.

Your Personal Business-Related Strengths will be particularly important if you own a Small-size company, but don't dismiss your importance in strategically leading your company, even if it is a Mid-size Or Large-size company. As a Strategic Business Leader, it's essential to your company's success that you use your Personal Business Related Strengths whether or not they are associated with what CEOs do in big public companies.

Consider how Bridget used her impressive selling ability to help her company achieve its sales goal. One day, she commented to her TAB Board, that her company had not hit its Company Plan's projected increased sales goals. In fact, she added, her company had actually experienced decreased sales over the previous two years. One of her TAB Board members asked her "what has happened in your company in the last two years that is different?" Bridget explained that she had cut back on the time she spent meeting with new accounts prospects to focus on other areas of the company that she considered more CEO in nature. Bridget's selling ability was responsible for many major accounts when her company was experiencing great growth. None of Bridget's sales employees, who had all been with the company for years, could close account sales the way she had done for many years. Therefore, her TAB Board recommended that she get involved again in selling, at least for the short-term, until her company's sales were back on track with projections. Within months of Bridget reallocating her work time so that she was spending 50%

of her time working with new account prospects, her company's sales were back on track with the company sales plan projections. At the same time, she also upgraded the caliber of her sales team with two new salespeople and she also invested in better sales training and tools for the salespeople.

The Personal Business-Related Weaknesses of many business owners have been a factor in their Company Plans not succeeding. For example, Andrew Arden has a Weakness that stood in the way of his Company Plans succeeding. He is an excellent "people person," but he could not take the tough actions that involved conflicts with employees. He not only does not like to deal with employee conflicts – he is also not very good at it. An example of this is when one of his project managers repeatedly failed to complete specific Tactics he had committed to doing in order to support the Company DCSF Plan. Yet, Andrew continued to employ the project manager without addressing the issue and without setting any consequences. Andrew's conflict avoidance in this matter kept Andrew's Company DCSF Plan from succeeding.

The breakthrough took place when Andrew's TAB Board advised him that he would have to learn how to neutralize this weakness. Andrew took their advice and decided to delegate employee conflict responsibilities to his office manager – a woman who had no problem dealing with such issues. The next day, the office manager informed the project manager of specific changes that would need to be made – immediately – or he would be out of a job. Ultimately, Andrew had to let go of the project manager. Two months later, the results for Andrew's Company DCSF Plan soared. If you have a leadership weakness, try to neutralize this weakness by delegating the responsibility to an employee who does not share this same weakness.

Mark Conroy has a leadership weakness that involves losing focus on his Company Plans before his Company Goals are reached. Mark gets very excited about new Company Plans, but then fails to stay on top of them. Mark is not alone in having this leadership weakness. Many successful business owners are more emotionally fit for a sprint than a marathon. They have great passion and excitement for change, but by nature, it is hard for them to keep an ongoing focus on making sure Company Plans succeed. To be an effective Strategic Business Leader, it is essential that you maintain focus on monitoring actual results versus projected results. In Mark's situation, he worked out a program with his Executive Assistant in which she would keep him focused on staying on top of monitoring results. She gave him daily and weekly reminders of set benchmarks to make the specifics of the Plans more down to earth and more urgent on a regular basis.

For some business owners, the Business-Related Opportunity may result in the business owner attending some industry training programs or even going back to college. Mark discussed with his TAB Board the fact that he had a weakness in the area of basic business knowledge. He was quite knowledgeable from the technical end, but in order for Conroy Technologies to become more successful, he felt he needed to obtain a MBA. His lack of basic business workings in the management end was his Weakness.

Your approach to leading your business may be affected by Personal Business-Related Threats outside your control. Andrew Arden's heart attacks created a need to commit time to train his project manager to take over some of his leadership responsibilities. This in turn helped counter the extreme stress at work, which was partially responsible for Andrew's health problems. It also gave his company protection, should he become incapacitated or die. As part of this solution, Andrew started holding weekly meetings with his project manager to keep each other abreast of everything they were working on relating to the Company Plan. This way, if anything happened to either of them, the other would know the full status of the Company Plan.

### WARNING:

There is a fine line between delegating too much – being extremely "hands-off" – and not delegating enough. The business owner walks a tightrope trying to balance this. Strategic Business Leaders need to delegate only after they determine that the Responsible Party for an Action Plan has first demonstrated the competency to do the Task. A common mistake is giving "ownership" to a manager as the Responsible Party for an important Action Plan before the manager has proven competency in handling Action Plans in nearly the same level of responsibility. It is important to test how well a manager does with lesser responsibility before turning over the responsibility for an important Action Plan.

# REVIEW AND MODIFY COMPANY ACTION PLANS FREQUENTLY

In order to keep my bicycle in top shape and working efficiently, I need to regularly check on basic things like the air pressure in my tires and proper brake alignment. Even though you may be taking your bike in once a year for a thorough check up, you also need to periodically check to make sure your bike is operating efficiently by checking the air pressure, tread, gears, brakes, etc. Your company Blueprint Bike must also be in good working condition. In the same way, you need to periodically pull over and take the time to make sure that the key parts of your Company Action Plans are working properly.

You are the catalyst for making your Company Plans succeed, and you're more likely to reach your destination of success if you include regularly scheduled Company Action Plan and Tactic reviews of the KPIs and time deadlines. These review meetings identify any Action Plan or Tactic results that are not tracking as projected, by reviewing the measurable results of the Tactics for that Action Plan. These regularly scheduled meetings will keep your employees focused on the KPIs for which they are responsible.

When your Action Plans are not achieving their projected results, there is something wrong. Like a flat tire, you have to fix the tire to move forward. The review of your Action Plan results may cause you to make changes to your Action Plans, or the Tactics of the Action Plan, if the results indicate that you are not on track toward your Goal.

These shifts in Tactics often make the difference as to whether your plans succeed or not. Regularly scheduled meetings to discuss the status of Tactics allow you to make changes in a timely manner. This use of review meetings is an important edge your business has over the competition that is not using Blueprint.

In a Small-size company like Arden Construction, Action Plan reviews might only occur monthly because of limited manpower. In a Mid-size company, like Baker Manufacturing, weekly or bi-weekly review meetings are much more common. In a Large-size company, like Conroy Technologies, there are enough managers with sufficient time to make sure that weekly Action Plan review meetings take place.

It is essential that these regularly scheduled Action Plan reviews are set like stone, as it is too easy for things to come up and for them to be put off. There will always be something. Regularly scheduled Action Plan reviews require a high level of commitment, self-discipline and self-accountability on your part as the Strategic Leader of your business.

## ONE-ON-ONE MEETINGS WITH RESPONSIBLE PARTY

As a Strategic Business Leader, it is important that you meet regularly, one-on-one, with every Responsible Party for a Company Action Plan. During these individual meetings, ask the Responsible Party to discuss actual results versus projected results and review timeline commitments. One TAB member owner of a Large-size company told me that one of his sales managers was giving him projected sales results and not designating them as such. The TAB member thought, "Wow, we are really doing well." That was until he found out that the sales manager was not giving him the actual results. By having regular meetings, the TAB member was able to realize the discrepancy. It may seem obvious, but make sure that you are getting actual results so that you can compare them to predicted results.

Feedback from the Responsible Parties often leads to modifications and revisions of the Tactics for which these employees are responsible. Their suggestions will often tap into creative ideas for suggested changes of Tactics, even Tactics that are not directly the responsibility of the employees giving the suggestions.

For instance, Bridget Baker color codes the actual versus predicted results with red if her Responsible Parties missed predicted results, yellow if they were close and green if the actual results met or exceeded the forecast. At her regularly scheduled meetings with the managers who are responsible for one of her company Action Plans, she asks them to explain to her why predicted results for those priorities in red were not achieved.

When meeting one-on-one with Responsible Parties for

the results of each Action Plan, it is important to ask them, as Bridget does, to explain why predicted results are not achieved. In addition, ask the following type questions for each of their Tactical commitments:

- What are the measured results of the Action Plan or Tactic compared to projected results?

- Are the projected results on track? (Yes or No)

- If the projected results of the Action Plan are not on track, which Tactics are not being completed on schedule?

- What caused the poor results? These reasons need to be understood before you try to overcome the roadblocks that stand in the way of success.

- If the project is not on track, what is needed to get on track?

- If the project can't get back on track, what is the new track and what is needed to hit and stay on this track?

## DEMONSTRATED PROGRESS

If you have assigned a task with a deadline date that has benchmarks, you need to go deeper than just being satisfied with a report from the party responsible for the Action Plan. Periodically, require the Responsible Party for an Action Plan to demonstrate to you the progress that has been made on the Action Plan, rather than just report the status.

Bridget had a major design project with a deadline for a customized fabrication that was to be completed by the beginning of June. The Action Plan had benchmarks dates for partial completion to take place by the previous March, April and May, which was committed to by the manager who was the Responsible Party. Literally, each week this employee said he was right on target. However, Bridget never took the step of asking the project manager to demonstrate for her the specific progress on the Plan. Weeks before the entire project was to be completed, the Responsible Party for an Action Plan fired an employee who was working on the Action Plan. The fired employee contacted Bridget to let her know that there was no way the project was going to be even partially completed by the due date. When Bridget asked the manager who was the Responsible Party for the Action Plan to give her a demonstration of the completed benchmark, the manager couldn't perform the demonstration because the project was greatly behind schedule. What Bridget learned from this experience was that when benchmarks are involved in tasks, she clearly needs to see evidence to see that the actual status is in line with reported status.

## COMPUTER GENERATED MEASUREMENT DASHBOARDS

As technology becomes more capable of measuring results, it is easy and inexpensive to use computer-generated measurement dashboards comparing projected KPI results versus actual KPI results. TAB's Business Builder's Blueprint web-based application includes a KPI tracking module which tracks each KPI and reports status as Green, Yellow or Red based on actual results compared to plan. You want to easily understand the status of each Tactic for your Action Plans. Dashboards provide a summary of the state of your Blueprint Plans on one page. Spending a very small amount of time to put in place this easily accessible technology will save you many hours of time and enable you to lead in an objective fashion based upon measurements.

## DO NOT PERMIT MOVING TIME TARGETS

Business owners should never assume things are going according to plan just because no one is volunteering to tell you that the results you expect are not happening. Whether you or one of your managers is responsible for a specific Action Plan, it is essential that you do not permit a culture in which missing deadlines for specific Tactics is acceptable. It will become a joke among your employees if they know they can give a completion date and then, when the date is missed, say, without repercussion that "It wasn't done, but I'll do it by," then giving a new completion date.

You must become the leadership force that ensures that the company makes timely revisions to your Company Action Plans when required. One of the keys to strategically leading your business is to not permit your Action Plan deadlines to be pushed back repeatedly, because they are so vital to the success of your Strategic Plans. A business owner should not sit back and do nothing about it when the business owner sees Action Plans or Tactics aren't being done to his or her satisfaction or in a timely manner.

A missed date is bound to happen, but it cannot become the

norm. You need to make it clear that completion dates do matter and are set in stone; you do this by establishing a company culture that sets a prime priority on completion dates. Doug Conroy used to allow his operations manager to continuously miss dates with no a set repercussions for those missed dates. This established a company culture in which other employees did not feel an urgency to meet their dates either. This dramatically set back the progress the company had been making towards achieving its DCSF Goal.

To get things back on track, Doug announced to his employees that missed dates would no longer be permitted. He made it clear that the Responsible Party for any Action Plan should think long and hard before agreeing to benchmark dates or completion dates. He added that once those dates were set, he expected them to be met. He established that it was a good practice to be ahead of the schedule rather than behind it.

Once this policy was put in place, his operations manager missed two different committed dates within the next 30 days. He wrote up a formal letter to go into the personnel file for the operations manager. This upset the operations manager who mentioned it to a few of Doug's other managers. Interestingly, all his managers began to give realistic deadlines that could be met. Even the operations manager began to make them every time.

This change that Doug made, in refusing to accept missed dates without consequences, became a mindset to which his managers strictly adhered. The implementation and backup and follow-through with repercussions are a crucial aspect of getting employees to take all deadlines seriously.

## CHAPTER TWENTY-THREE

## STRATEGIC BUSINESS LEADERS ARE NOT AFRAID TO REPLACE UNPRODUCTIVE PERSONNEL

Strategic Business Leaders do an objective evaluation of whether they have the right talent on board to achieve the Company Vision Statement. You need the right people doing the right jobs. If you don't have the right people, you need to replace them with those who are best suited for the job. Business owners often have a tendency to overlook or rationalize away the deficiencies of some personnel because of an emotional attachment to the person or because they have invested time in that person. If the problem is that a key manager or other employee doesn't have 'the stuff,' whether it is ability or attitude, you must act, even if it means taking a step backwards temporarily. I believe it is sometimes better to cut your losses than to hold onto someone who is not allowing the company to move forward.

Bridget determined that her Company DCSF Plan was not going to succeed while she had the wrong sales manager. It was difficult to let the sales manager go because she really liked him as a person; he simply was not the right person for the job. She addressed this situation by hiring a new sales manager and, because she didn't want to fire the sales manager, instead offered him a demotion back to a sales role. Within a few months, the new sales manager was getting better results and her demoted sales manager excelled at what he had always been good at – selling.

# USE FEEDBACK FROM EMPLOYEES AT ALL LEVELS

One of the most effective ways to get feedback from your employees on specific Action Plans is through regularly scheduled meetings with specific groups of employees involved in specific Company Action Plans. Your Company Action Plans are much more likely to succeed if you get ideas and other feedback from your employees relating to the Tactics assigned to them. For these group meetings to be most beneficial, make your Action Plan information accessible to everyone to whom the information is applicable. Leave out those parts that may be politically charged and not suitable for sharing.

Too many business leaders never learn about powerful suggestions because those suggestions never made it up the ranks up to the leader. There are many reasons why these suggestions don't make it to the leader. Sometimes, those who are lower on the employment scale do not feel that they can approach the business leader or even their immediate managers. In other instances, immediate managers may not see the value in the suggestions and therefore not pass them on up. Sometimes immediate managers will not want to pass on the ideas because it may "show them up."

A company culture must be established in which suggestions are welcome. Once employees know their suggestions are welcome, they will feel a greater sense of buy-in to what will make the company succeed. It is hard for some leaders to hear their employees challenge their strategies. One way to accomplish this is to hold scheduled group meetings during which employees can ask questions, make suggestions and express their views. Scheduling this type of group meeting will emphasize that you value their views. For some of your employees, the group setting will reduce the stress factor of being asked for feedback that they might otherwise feel during a one-on-one session with the business owner.

Doug Conroy has brought about important changes to his Company Plan, which has helped bring about success, by periodically meeting with mid-level and front line employees to tap into their ideas and thinking. He makes sure that their department heads are present at these meetings, so that he is not viewed as undermining the authority of his department heads. During meetings with these employees, Doug asks why they think certain specific projected results aren't tracking as projected. These meetings often result in information that has not been brought up to Doug by managers, even though they may have been aware of these ideas. At first, employees were reluctant to voice their opinions, suggestions and constructive criticism. Doug was disappointed and tried to figure out how to get the employees to become more open.

He started meeting one-on-one with certain employees who had been in their departments for quite a while. He asked them why so many employees were reluctant to express their ideas during the group meetings he had just conducted. They told him that they had been shut down in the past. They simply didn't believe that anything would be done about any of their ideas. In response, Doug scheduled the next round group meetings with the same employees. But this time he gave his personal assurance that they would not have to worry about any retaliation if they expressed ideas to the managers.

He let these employees know that their feedback mattered to him and that he would try to quickly implement the ideas he felt could be helpful to the company. After listening to the ideas expressed by these employees during the second round of group meetings, he was quick to bring about follow-up changes. Whenever Doug feels that he can't use an employee volunteered idea, he follows up with an email to the employee giving the recommendation and respectfully explains why he didn't use it. In some cases, while the ideas for changes to the Action Plans may have been good, the timing was wrong. In such cases, he let the employee making the suggestions know that the changes had to be put off for several months in order to be effective.

## KNOW HOW TO RUN GROUP MEETINGS

For optimum atmosphere of openness and effectiveness at any meeting, one-on-one or group meetings, all employees should agree/ adhere to/have an understanding of the following:

- **Interruptions are only for emergencies.**

- Comments should not be given in a way that they stifle others from giving their views.

- Verbal attacks are prohibited.

- Being defensive is not productive.

- This is not the place for raised voices or yelling.

- All cell phones should be turned off; there should be neither ringing nor texting.

Be sensitive to the fact that Responsible Parties for Action Plans may be trying to look good in front of you; therefore, they often will have excuses as to why the Action Plan isn't being achieved (being defensive). Meetings can be bogged down with these kinds of excuses and defensiveness. Be an efficient facilitator by making sure attendees do not share too many details and spend an inordinate amount of time discussing minutiae. It is your responsibility as the leader to keep attendees on track.

Use eye contact and attentive body language while leading these meetings. It is also a good communication skill to paraphrase what they are saying by summarizing when needed. Synthesize what they are saying. Prompt quiet attendees to participate by asking them specific questions. This is one of the most important techniques you possess in making the meetings productive. Employ the Socratic method of questioning by asking questions that beget well-thought out answers. Test assumptions. Use the time to gather information and find hidden points by probing.

It is best to ask "why" questions instead of questions that call for "yes" or "no" answers. Be sure to ask "why" things are not going as planned. But this is not the time to blame or confront, which can be counterproductive to creativity.

Also, ask "what" and "how" type questions to elicit fresh ideas that could improve your current Company Action Plans or possibly create new plans. Answers to these questions will help determine what needs to be modified. Get the team to build on one another's thoughts to ensure that the ideas represent collective thinking.

## DON'T WASTE EMPLOYEE TIME IN MEETINGS

One of the biggest complaints employees have about meetings is the wasted time. No employee should have to attend an entire group meeting if the employee is only going to be involved in a small percentage of the topics being discussed at the meeting. It is very common, for example, for a Director of Technology or a General Counsel, to be called into a group meeting when issues regarding either technology or legalities are on the agenda.

## WHAT MEETINGS DO YOU NEED TO ATTEND

The larger your company, the more likely the Responsible Party for an Action Plan will assign certain Tactics in the Action Plan to subordinate employees. Each Responsible Party for an Action Plan needs to schedule weekly reviews with the subordinate or subordinates who have been charged with making the Tactics succeed. Although popping in on them in a non-predictable fashion may bring you insight on what is actually happening, you don't need to be present at all of these meetings. Most of the time, it will be sufficient if the

Responsible Parties provides a short summary update on how the Action Plan is progressing, without going into detail about the status of each of the Tactics.

# COMMUNICATING FOR RESULTS

There are a couple of techniques to incorporate in your leadership approach that will help bring about greater company results. One of the communication techniques involves the promotion of companywide support of your Company DCSF Goal(s). The second technique involves bringing about an openness of communications that creates, what I will explain to you later, a safe TABenos atmosphere.

## COMMUNICATION TECHNIQUES FOR PROMOTING COMPANYWIDE SUPPORT OF YOUR COMPANY DCSF PLAN GOAL(S)

Regardless of the size of your company, you will need to develop a strategy for promoting awareness and getting support for your company's DCSF Plan Goal(s). This awareness must reach everyone in your company so that the whole company is on the same page. They will all need to see – and understand – the benefits to the company when the DCSF Goal(s) is achieved.

One of your main communications objectives should be geared towards bringing about a culture that supports your Company DCSF Goal(s). It should reach every department and every employee at every level. When everybody in the department knows the Goal(s) of the DCSF Plan, it is much more likely that the department will take ownership of those areas of the DCSF Plan the department is responsible for completing.

Your methods for making sure every one of your employees knows the Goal(s) of your Company DCSF Plan may involve using tools such as e-mails, motivational and personal presentations and videos to bring about the excitement needed to get employee focus. You may want to develop visual reminders of the DCSF Goal(s) and progress in the forms of signs or graphs and they should be placed on your company walls

Baker Manufacturing, for example, displayed its DCSF Goal on posters, which were displayed in the lunchrooms for the office workers and the factory workers. These posters simply stated, "Increase Company gross profits by 3 percent by end of this year."

It is helpful to get feedback from certain key employees before communicating the Company Plan to all others involved. Make sure this is received from employees you trust for this type of feedback. To help you determine the best way to communicate your Company DCSF Plan Goal(s) throughout your company, answer the following questions:

- **Who should do the communicating? It may be you, or you may decide to delegate this responsibility.**

- **What level of details of the Company DCSF Plan**

Goal(s) do you want to share?

- What methods and tools of communication will be most effective to clearly express the company DCSF Plan Goal(s) information to all the relevant parties?

- Should the communications be virtual or tangible?

- At what physical location(s) should the communication take place if your company has several locations or more than one meeting area in your location?

- With what size groups should you meet? Effective communication may not be possible with too big a group. Meeting with smaller groups using different communication methods may prove more effective.

- Do you want to open the meetings to discussions by employees relating to the company DCSF Plan Goal(s), and if so, what format should you use for facilitating the group discussions?

No matter how clearly you communicate your DCSF Plan Goal(s), some employees will think, "That's great – it's going to be more work for us and more profits for the owners, and the executives will get bigger bonuses." You have the power to neutralize this misunderstanding by creating employee rewards that can be earned when the DCSF Goal(s) is achieved or clear benchmarks towards the DCSF Goal(s) are achieved.

Baker Manufacturing identified department-related Critical

Success Factor Statements for every department that had any part in making its Company DCSF Plan succeed. For each quarter that an individual department reached its benchmark, different rewards were given, none of which exceeded $50.00 per employee.

For example, when Mark Conroy announced the Conroy Company DCSF Plan Goal to his employees, he let them know that they would each receive a dinner for two, at any one of six specific restaurants, if the company achieved its DCSF Goal within the stated timeline. He also announced less expensive company-wide rewards, such as baseball tickets, for quarterly benchmarks met along the way toward achieving the company DCSF Plan Goal. Mark used graphs that he had posted in the company lunchrooms, which showed the benchmarks needed every three months in order to be on track to achieve the Company DCSF Plan Goal by its targeted completion date.

## CREATING A SAFE COMMUNICATION "TABENOS" COMPANY ENVIRONMENT

One of the keys to using communications for getting greater results is the existence of an atmosphere at your company in which your employees feel it is safe to communicate their thoughts. At TAB, we use a methodology that we call, "TABenos," to avoid counter-productive business communication and instead encourage a communication atmosphere in which all employees feel safe and comfortable. TABenos is an extrapolation of a safe communication atmosphere that existed in Greek mythology, which referred to "temenos." Some feel temenos translates to "sanctuary." "Temenos" is, in Greek mythology, a place where warriors could feel safe and put down their armor and defenses.

We use TABenos exercises, which I will explain in more detail shortly, within our corporate office TAB meetings and teach our TAB members how to do the same with their companies. The objective is to create an environment where employees can express their views in an open and honest manner. TABenos helps eliminate negative communication behaviors such as negative tone and raised voices. It also helps people feel that their ideas are valuable.

The TABenos system begins with the business owner meeting with key employees. The business leader explains that the purpose of this meeting is to develop an understanding of how to successfully communicate, where the environment allows for safe, honest and open communication.

TABenos meetings have to be facilitated by a facilitator who will call on each participant in the meeting to respond to a few TABenos exercise questions. Each of the participants will give their responses to the questions, using one word or a small phrase. The facilitator then writes and displays the responses to these questions.

The first exercise involves the facilitator asking the participants to list what each person believes to be defensive communication. What communication actions may cause them or others to "don their armor"? For example, is someone using sarcasm, avoiding eye contact, being silent, responding defensively, changing the subject, making cynical remarks, objecting or outright lying?

The second thing they are asked to do is to describe what a "safe, honest and open" communication environment looks like. Some good answers are: there are no hidden agendas, people respect all ideas, participants find common grounds, positive feedback or positive criticism is given, and appreciation is shown for the communication attempts.

The third question participants are asked is to come up with a list of benefits that will be gained when communicating in a safe and open TABenos communication environment. Some examples are members who express that they feel safe to learn from each other, get more ideas from each other, gain a support system and feel as if they can build trust and also bond with one another.

The fourth step involves buy-in and commitment. The facilitator asks the participants to look at each of the responses to the previous questions. They need to ask for any clarification or express any disagreements they may have with anything so far. From this, the list will undergo a certain amount of tweaking.

After the wording has been clarified and deletions have been made, the facilitator will ask participants for a verbal commitment to adhere to the TABenos culture when communicating with each other. This is done by calling "TABenos" on anyone violating the agreed-upon TABenos culture. The facilitator will explain that each participant is responsible for pointing out any future displays of armor or communication that causes armor to appear.

Doing the TABenos exercises provides more benefits to a company than just improved communication. It has often been carried over into owners' and employees' non-business communications. One TAB member we worked with was an owner who was having difficulty communicating with his daughter, an attorney. After implementing the TABenos system, they found the biggest benefit was the improvement in the way they began to communicate with each other outside of the business.

It is important to review the TABenos system annually. Things can change for some employees. Some communication patterns formed within the year might not have been present before, or dynamics have changed because new employees are now involved. Periodically, the results of the company TABenos exercises should be distributed to members of the group who have committed to TABenos. The following is an example of the results of a TABenos exercise at Conrad Technologies.

## TABENOS COMMITMENT

We, the management group for Conroy Technologies, have discussed the desire to create a communications group atmosphere in which everyone feels safe and comfortable in expressing their views in an open manner, so each manager will help other managers to greater personal and business success. Together our discussions have discovered the following conditions, which may exist and agree to recognize the following:

## CONDITIONS WHICH CONTRIBUTE TO THE RAISING OF ARMOR TO PREVENT EFFECTIVE COMMUNICATIONS:

- Non- participation

- Purposely wasting time

- Contrarian always-in-opposition opinions

- Illogical, unemotional responses

- Pedantic

## CHAPTER TWENTY-FIVE

- Being late to meetings

- Dishonesty

- Exaggeration

- Public criticism (berating)

- Negativity creating barriers

- No discussion

- Overemotional responses

- Intentional deception

- Pettiness

- Questioning ethics and sincerity

- Uneducated responses

- Condescending responses

- Hollow excuses

- Mistrust

- Personal Attacks

**AFTER DISCUSSION OUR GROUP HAS AGREED THE FOLLOWING CONDITIONS HAVE TO BE PRESENT AT MEETINGS FOR OUR MANAGERS TO FEEL SAFE, HONEST AND OPEN:**

- Absence of hidden agendas

- Know each other (develops over time)

- Sincerity

- Trust

- Openness

- Neutral environment

- No Fear

- Guidelines for conduct

- Non-judgmental atmosphere

- Goal Oriented discussions

- Win-Win Atmosphere

**OUR GROUP DISCUSSIONS HAVE IDENTIFIED THE FOLLOWING BENEFITS BY USING TABENOS:**

- Foundation to build upon

- Greater effort

- Build trust

- New and creative ideas

- Greater understanding

- Personal growth

- Increased leadership development

- Businesses will run more effectively

- Resolution of problems

- Better understanding of problems

- Group Growth

- Synergy

- Reduction of common stress

- Working together towards our common goals

**WE AGREE TO "CALL TABENOS" ON ANYBODY WHO VIOLATES THE TABENOS COMMUNICATIONS COMMITMENT AT COMPANY MEETINGS.**

## CHAPTER 26

# LEADERSHIP TEAM TO HELP MAKE IT HAPPEN

Many Large-size companies designate a group of managers who meet regularly to monitor results of their Company Blueprint Action Plans. This group is typically called a "Leadership Team," although some companies refer to them as "Planning Teams." If you are a Large-size company, you should create a Leadership Team to review and modify your Action Plans, including the Tactics for each Action Plan, as needed to make your Company Plans succeed.

## SELECTING LEADERSHIP TEAM MEMBERS

One of the key roles of your Leadership Team members is to challenge your Company Action Plans and Tactics. They are not meant to blindly agree with everything you do. Pick members who will openly and honestly express their views. Don't make the mistake of choosing Leadership Team members who are "rubber stamps" or "yes" people. Your Leadership Team members must feel comfortable to share different views about your Company Blueprint Statements.

Leadership Team members should never include any employee who reports to any other member of the Leadership Team. Consider, for example, the potential conflict and disruption to your Leadership Team if both your Vice President of Marketing and your Director of Marketing, who reports to your Vice President of Marketing, were to be on your Leadership Team.

Your Leadership Team should be limited to a small number, ideally not more than six company executives, who report directly to you, if you are also the COO of your company, or to your company COO if you are not the COO of your company. Other executives and managers will be invited to attend portions of Leadership Team meetings, as needed, to share their views and provide their feedback on specific business areas.

## CONCENTRIC CIRCLES OF FEEDBACK WITH YOUR INFORMAL EXTERNAL ADVISORS

Your Leadership Team is not a substitute for feedback from your informal external advisors, such as your TAB Board. They are not intended to advise you how to lead your business more effectively. Instead, the relationship between your informal external advisors and Leadership Team can be thought of as concentric circles of feedback. The first circle of feedback, which is the closer circle, will come from your informal strategic advisors, if you have them. Your Leadership Team is the other circle. After you get advice from your informal strategic advisors, you may want to share the advice with your Leadership Team to get their thoughts.

YOU

INFORMAL STRATEGIC ADVISORS

MANAGEMENT TEAM

### LEADERSHIP TEAM ROLE IN HELPING TO MAKE IT HAPPEN!

Your Leadership Team members must clearly understand their roles as Team members and they must be fully committed to the Blueprint process. To bring about this clarity, consider developing a Leadership Team charter, such as the following one that Conrad Technology Company uses.

*"To facilitate success, you, as a member of the Leadership Team, need self-discipline, perseverance and an ability to focus on what is most important for Conrad Technology Company ... You must direct your energies to satisfying Conrad Technology Company's Critical Success Factors, particularly the Driving Critical Success Factor. No matter how many important day-to-day areas need to be addressed, you have to focus on those areas that impact the Driving Critical Success Factor most. This focus will give you improved, directed energy that will increase your productivity in areas that lead Conrad Technology Company toward its Company Vision Statement."*

## CHAPTER TWENTY-SIX

## FACILITATING LEADERSHIP TEAM MEETING

There are many challenges with facilitating Leadership Team meetings. One of the challenges of facilitating a Leadership Team meeting is preventing a "yes-man" effect by making it clear that you welcome and expect challenges to the ideas you express at the meeting. Use the TABenos exercises to ensure that there is an open, safe atmosphere. Make sure the meeting starts and ends on time and that you control the pace of the Leadership Team meeting. It is also important that Leadership Team meetings don't get off track.

The facilitator's ability to get the most value from your Operation Team members is enhanced if the facilitator has an understanding of the natural behavioral style of each member of the team. There are many inexpensive tools that can be used to determine behavioral style. If you learn the behavioral profiles of each Leadership Team member, you will be best able to communicate in a way with each member that best fits their behavioral nature. For example, a team member with a personality/behavior that is not a very dominant type may need more encouragement to open up with his or her views. On the flip side, your challenge in facilitating a person with a very dominant type of behavior may require you to remind the member to not dominate the meeting and instead to allow others to speak.

Facilitate in a way that emphasizes the importance of prioritizing and focusing on thoughts and ideas, rather than getting bogged down in details. Acknowledge different recommendations and optional actions. Pay attention to timelines so that you do not spend too much time on one item, without having time for other important items to discuss.

Most Leadership Team meetings are scheduled for only two hours at the same set time and day of the month, each month. However, some Large-size companies have the management depth to allocate more time for the Leadership Team meetings. Conroy Technologies, for example, has weekly Leadership Team meetings of four hours from 8:30 a.m. to 12:30 p.m., every Wednesday, to track the status of each listed Tactic in each Action Plan.

Your Leadership Team's meeting should allocate needed time to focus on your Company DCSF Plan. Any remaining time, during the regularly scheduled meetings, should be spent on other Company Plans, but only if there is time left at the end of the meeting.

Your Leadership Team is going to be on top of reviewing and revising, as needed, the Company Action Plans, including the Tactics for making the plans succeed. Leadership Teams review the specific results of Company Plans, particularly the Company DCSF Plan, at each Leadership Team meeting. To do this, the complete Action Plan information of every Company Plan needs to be accessible to all the members of your Company Leadership Team. Reviewing results of all your Company Plans will keep your Leadership Team informed of things outside their areas of responsibility, and also make them more accountable for things within their responsibility.

For Company Plans other than the Company DCSF Plan, the party responsible for these other Company Plans, which are typically being handled by a company team or department, should allocate time at the Leadership Team meetings for an update. Your Leadership Team members may have some questions that need to be answered by the Responsible Party, as well as suggestions for changes.

Even though the focus of your regularly scheduled review

meetings should be directed primarily to making your Company DCSF Plan happen, it may be very valuable at times for you to periodically ask department heads or team leaders responsible for other Company Plans to give you an overview status report of their progress.

If you bring in several of your managers into a group meeting to discuss the results versus projected results, you should expect different viewpoints, some of which can be very emotional. It is important that you reinforce your managers' respect for each other's views. At the end of the meeting, point out what you see as the priorities for the next review meeting, to help the team maintain its focus and momentum.

ELEMENT 4:
# CONCLUSION

You are pedaling hard to power your Blueprint Bicycle to attain the company success you desire, while you're steering your handlebars so that your Front Wheel takes you right to the Personal Vision of success that you dream. I have given you the tools and the techniques for strategically leading your business, while riding your unique Blueprint Bicycle. You know how to get you Blueprint Bicycle tuned-up so that you can enjoy a very successful ride as you strategically lead your company on its journey to success and reaching your personal dreams for your future.

Regardless of the size of your company or the state of the economy, never stop planning for the big dreams you want for the future of your company. You are the catalyst for change in your company. It's your business. You are at the controls, and the destination of your company is up to you. You are the one who must ingrain the importance of Blueprint into your company's culture.

As with any journey, there are bound to be rough spots and even unexpected detours in reaching your dreams. But your Blueprint Bicycle wheels will keep turning and moving your company toward the direction of your Company Vision. Using the Blueprint process creates timely strategic change that will power your company's journey to achieve the future you desire.

It is my sincere hope that you will use Business Builder's Blueprint to realize your Personal and Company Visions of success, just as it has done for the thousands of TAB business owner members worldwide who are using Blueprint.

*Allen Fishman*
*Founder of The Alternative Board*